The Railway Navvies of Set

C000262124

The story of the navvies wh
to build the Settle and C

by Sarah Lister, artwork by Teresa Gordon

Contents

"We read in the papers of great men who, by their feats of engineering, find a niche in the Temples of Fame; directing by their superior minds the labour of the humbler worker. Yet how few notice the hard working, hard eating and hard drinking navvy who has been an important element in maturing the project of his more richly endowed brother, and without whom all the brain power in the world would be of no avail", Chambers' Journal, 1872

This book is dedicated to the memory of all the navvies who worked on the Settle and Carlisle Railway, particularly those who sacrificed their lives.

Foreword

Passengers who journey on the seventy-two miles of railway between Settle and Carlisle can admire the breathtaking scenery of the Yorkshire Dales and the pastoral landscape of the Eden Valley in Cumbria. But spare a thought for the men who built the iron road over which modern trains travel effortlessly. These men were called 'navvies'. There are fifteen tunnels, twenty-four viaducts, twenty stations and over three hundred bridges over or under the railway. Each brick and stone was laid by hand.

Men, women and children lived in temporary communities: 'navvy camps' or 'shanty towns'. There was an extensive supply chain providing bricks, wood, building materials, horses, food and drink. When the railway was finished the navvies moved on to new jobs, often building other railways. But some did not move on. They gave up their lives so that today we can travel from Settle to Carlisle. Those who died are buried in graveyards along the line; some have headstones, many do not.

The story of the men, women and children who were left behind deserves to be told. In this book Sarah Lister has brought to life some of these people. It is astonishing how much information is available, if we only take the trouble to look for it. This is what Sarah has done with diligence and painstaking research. She reveals the hidden stories that have remained hidden in Settle for 150 years. I hope this work encourages others to research these hidden lives, and to reflect on the human endeavour that created one of the world's greatest railway lines.

Bryan Gray CBE DL
Chairman, Settle and Carlisle Railway Trust

Introduction — the navvies in Settle churchyard

On a sunny summer evening at Settle Parish Church, visitors are enjoying the 'Saints and Sinners' graveyard tour. But, as usual, the tour is interrupted by a steam train, on this occasion pulled by Tornado, speeding over the viaduct. The passengers wave down, as they always do. This is one of the joys of life in 21st century Settle.

The country's most scenic railway was one of the last to be built because of the technical challenges it presented. It was an 'engineering triumph' completed by 'pick and shovel' and exploiting 50 years' railway building wisdom and experience. It was built by the Midland Railway as a trunk route to lucrative Scottish trade, to overcome difficulties with a rival company's hold over the Ingleton Branch Line. There would be 14 tunnels and 22 viaducts built over 72 miles of hostile terrain in (typically) appalling weather conditions. A review in 1876 said the Settle and Carlisle Railway *"has given more trouble to the contractors...than any recently made in this country ... however the Midland engineers induced themselves to attempt its construction is a puzzle. It is emphatically a line of embankments, viaducts, cuttings and tunnels"*. One journalist wrote, *"There was not a level bit of ground between Settle and Carlisle large enough to build a house upon."*

Over 3000 navvies from all over the UK and Ireland worked on the construction of the line. It was a relatively well paid, but dangerous job. Across the country, there were thought to be at least three navvy deaths per mile of railway laid in areas of landscape such as this. The church graveyards along the route contain hundreds of these casualties, the majority of them buried without gravestones. The deaths were regarded as the inevitable consequence of an empire-leading engineering project. Few people recognised the navvies' transformational achievements at the time. Astute Elizabeth Garnett [H], co-founder of the Navvy Mission Society, was one of those who did; *"Certainly, no men in all the world so improve their country as navvies do in England. Their work will last for ages and if the world remains so long, people will come in hundreds of years to look and wonder at what they have done."* Indeed, we are doing just that.

The Parish Churches of Holy Ascension in Settle and St Leonard's in Chapel-le-Dale were the two selected to house identical plaques dedicated to the memory of the navvies who died in accidents during the building of the railway between Settle and Dent. Research has identified burials of 215 navvies and their families in Chapel-le-

Dale graveyard, 72 in the graveyard of St John's, Cowgill near Dent and 25 at St Mary's, Mallerstang towards Kirkby Stephen. So there are likely to be burials of navvies in Settle churchyard, but how many were there?

It's taken 150 years to find out.

Since 2018, **Settle Graveyard Project** has been researching the lives of those buried in the graveyard of Settle Parish Church. The railway was built through the open fields below the church and now the graveyard nestles below the railway embankment. The deaths between 1869 and 1876 raised intriguing questions about the men who made the ultimate sacrifice during the building of the railway. The Friends of the Settle-Carlisle Line (FoSCL) kindly paid for their death certificates to find out what happened.

- 20 navvies and two young apprentices died during the building of the railway.
- There were 30 more burials who were navvies' infants, children, mothers and wives.
- 7 navvies are commemorated with a gravestone. One gravestone names two navvies. One navvy was buried in a family plot at Giggleswick, although he was a Settle resident.

These men were not just another appalling statistic; every navvy was someone's son and possibly a husband and father. In the spirit of the Graveyard Project we owe it to their descendants and relations to find out who they were and celebrate the contribution they made to this iconic railway and to life in Settle.

This project has been humbling and some findings have been grim but they also provide a fascinating insight into life in Settle during the 19th century. Perhaps things today aren't so bad?! The accounts of these families provide a snapshot of navvy life and death which will probably have been repeated at each of the graveyards along the route. When you have read this booklet, please spare a thought and raise a toast to these incredible men, their achievements and their families.

Sarah Lister, November 2020

The navvies arrive in Settle

The quiet market town of Settle had never seen anything like this before, nor since! The railway transformed everyday life in Settle. Farmers could transport livestock quickly without marching them across the fells. Businesses could respond to demand as never before and new businesses sprang up. Even Settle could have a fish and chip shop! *[LSA]* With the Bank Holidays Act of 1872 there could be family visits and trips just for leisure. There were exciting 'excursion trains' to the coast for workers and groups such as the Temperance Society and Sunday Schools. Inevitably the coaching inns and drovers became casualties of the new railway trade. Of course, there was incredible disruption for several years while it was being built, but, overall, the gains outweighed the pains.

David Hearsum,

FISH and .

CHIP SALOON,

Wholesale Potato Dealer

The Folly, SETTLE.

⊹⊱⊰⊹

Good Accommodation for Tourists

HOT and COLD BATHS.

There are pros and cons to all developments. Think of the debates about HS2. The railways through Settle were no different. Parliamentary approval was given for the building of the Settle and Carlisle railway in 1866 but political wrangling delayed the start of the works until 1869 *[SC]*.

MIDLAND RAILWAY.—EXTENSION TO CARLISLE. — We understand the local opposition to this branch has been withdrawn. There can not be much doubt that the act will be passed in the next session, altho' strong opposition may be expected from rival companies. Altho' the main object of this line is to give the Midland greater facilities for commanding through traffic, one of its minor advantages will be to open an extensive district which has hitherto been practically unapproachable.

In May 1875 newspapers reflected that *"3000 labourers have long been engaged with steady perseverance in overcoming natural difficulties which at times seemed hopeless and insurmountable. Now that the heavy work has been got over, all concerned may fairly be congratulated upon the substantial and thorough style in which it has been done. At Settle itself the new line is sure to produce a change which will rather astonish some of the older inhabitants"* [2].

Under the general direction of these gentlemen, about three thousand labourers have long been engaged with steady perseverance in overcoming natural difficulties which at times seemed hopeless and insurmountable. Now that the heavy work has been got over, all concerned may fairly be congratulated upon the substantial and thorough style in which it has been done. At Settle itself the new line is sure to produce a change which will rather astonish some of the older inhabitants. The progress of railway works in the vicinity has already more or less disturbed the former repose of its streets, and ere long the place will be further enlivened by the arrival and departure of trains at a commodious new station in the village, instead of only at the old one, which is more than a mile distant. Well-built cottages are already springing up in the immediate neighbourhood of the new station, and ere long still further improvements may no doubt be looked for, in keeping with the spirit of the times.

The building of Contract No.1, the 'Long Drag', up from Settle Junction to Dent Head was achieved through the exertions of 2300 navvies and 130 horses. Most of these men had travelled from far afield so had unusual accents and weren't afraid to use *'brute force'* and *'fistic encounters'* (fighting with fists — fisticuffs) to settle an argument, destroying *'the quietude of our peaceful community'[CH]*.

There was a stigma attached to navvies, justified by the numerous reports of assault, drunken behaviour, and theft [1]. Generally, whilst the railway itself was welcomed, the navvy, his wife and children weren't [C].

—*Assault.*—John Ralph, of Settle, who had been apprehended under a warrant on the 25th instant, and admitted to bail by J. Birkbeck, Esq. on the following morning, appeared to answer a charge of having assaulted John Ornedge, a railway labourer at Settle. The hearing of the case occupied the Court for three hours, the result being that Ralph was fined 10s. and costs 19s. 6d., or in default fourteen days' imprisonment with hard labour.

The very name 'navvy' has passed into a synonym for all that is rough and uncouth; but although it is not far from the truth, there are 'navvies' and navvies.

The making of the Settle and Carlisle Railway was a very important event in the history of Settle. It brought into the town and neighbourhood an alien population, and soon after operations began the voice of the Cockney was heard in the land. Huts were erected to house the workmen and their families, a " Tommy Shop " was established in an old barn at the bottom of Duke Street to supply food, etc., and there were scenes of bustle and excitement in the somnolent little town.

As a rule the newcomers were well behaved, but occasionally quarrels arose which led to fights in the fields outside the town. Such fistic encounters as these took place were practically unknown in Settle, and I can recall several ghastly exhibitions which we youngsters witnessed with horror. The contestants, stripped to the waist, faced each other in a ring formed by partisans and other spectators, and then began a display of brute force, which in some instances, both were incapacitated and covered with blood. It was not an edifying spectacle, and I merely mention it to show how an alien element were able to destroy the quietude of our peaceful community.

Occasionally offences were more serious. **Christopher Wright**, aged 75, with only one (left) arm ran the Bay Horse beerhouse in Langcliffe. **Ellis Parker/Nelson**, a London navvy, was *"under the influence of liquor"* and wouldn't leave after the landlady refused him more alcohol [1]. He started fighting with Christopher who fell and hit his head on furniture with fatal results. Surgeon *William Altham* cared for Christopher until he died. A report from the trial explained that, as Ellis did not use a weapon to attack Christopher, he was only guilty of manslaughter, rather than murder and so imprisoned for five years with hard labour. The license of the Bay Horse was revoked although it still sold beer at the time of following censuses. It changed its name to the 'Pig and Whistle'.

Without clean drinking water available, liquor was routinely drunk for sustenance, rehydration and relaxation, sometimes with fatal consequences. Up at the Batty Wife settlement, where hundreds of navvies lived, the Midland Railway paid for clergy, ministers and educators to work

CHARGE OF MURDER AT SETTLE.—Ellis Parker *alias* Nelson, who had been, up to the time of his apprehension, employed on the new Settle and Carlisle line of railway, now in course of construction, was again brought up on remand on Wednesday, before Mr. J. Birkbeck, Rev. H. J. Swale, and Mr. H. Christie, charged with having, on the 9th inst., maliciously and wilfully, with malice aforethought, maltreated Christopher Wright, a beerseller, at Langcliffe, near Settle, from the effects of which he died on the 16th inst. A Coroner's inquest was held on the 17th inst., before Mr. T. P. Brown, deputy-coroner, when a verdict of manslaughter was returned. The deceased was 75 years old. The prisoner, who made no statement, was committed for trial.

"to divert the mens [sic] attention from pursuits and places of corrupting character"! Several of Settle's middle classes went to help. There was even a reading room and a library with 150 books and newspapers:

"The room for reading and entertainments is provided gratuitously by Mr. Ashwell (the contractor) *for the benefit of the men on the railway works and has been fitted up with books, periodicals etc, by public subscriptions. Through the benevolent exertions and liberality of the Rev. Mr. Pierson, (the vicar of Settle church)...the workmen have the privilege of reading and being instructed in writing, arithmetic, and other branches of an English education gratis"* [A].

These efforts weren't always appreciated by the navvies!

Hide from the Devil [F]

> *His woman's got religion, it changed her overnight*
> *Now she's reading scripture, quotes from the Bible, every time they fight*
> *She tells him he's a drunkard, won't let him have his way*
> *Until he gives up on the drinking, on the bed her side she'll stay*

> *Chorus: You can hide from the devil, run from your wife*
> *But never let the Temperance League get you in their sights*
> *They'll descend upon you like a flock of angry crows*
> *I'd sooner he fight ten Navvy lads, than deal with the likes of those*

> *The man she knew he fell asleep, head on the railway track*
> *He was drunk as drunk as drunk could be, now he's never coming back*
> *Train came through in the middle of the night, driver never saw him lyin'*
> *Sleepin' it off on a railway track is a sure way of dyin'*

> *His woman's gone and left him, for a navvy half her age*
> *She met him at her Bible class, says he has been saved*
> *Not a drop of liquor, all his wages she receives*
> *I swear to God he'll help him pray, when he knocks him to his knees*

Of course, some navvies, such as **John Owen,** made a valuable contribution to the life of the town. Settle town provided the base for operations at the southern end of the line. The station sidings and Ashfield area housed numerous temporary white washed wooden sheds, stables and (primitive) machinery.

"The railway yard, which is a little on the east side of Settle, is a place of much excitement on account of the various occupations going on. The ringing of anvils, the hammering of carpenters, the tramp of heavy horses, the puffing, steaming and whistling of locomotives, the different keyed voices of workmen, the clang of cutting, grinding,

crushing and sawing machinery and the quick motions of persons on business, all tended to give the place an aspect of unusual activity and restlessness. The railway yard included within its wooden precincts a saddler's shop, a carpenter's shop, saw mill, store rooms, a 7-flued smithy, numerous wooden huts, and two stables fit up for 40 horses. The stables were very clean and the few horses that were there were in excellent condition." [A]

"It is the dinner hour and a strange silence prevails throughout the works. Navvies are taking their siesta on the great piled-up baulks of timber, in various and grotesque attitudes; apparently sleeping as composedly, and certainly snoring as satisfactorily as any alderman could hope to do on his feather bed; while ever and anon some foreman or mason comes to his wooden cottage door, and wistfully gazes at the strangers" [B]

Shortly after its start from this point, the line crosses the Skipton road by a fine skew girder bridge, 62 feet span, passing on the left Auley House, the residence of Mr. John Birbeck. It then enters a deep cutting through gritstone, from which many of the bridges have been built, and crosses the turnpike road by another handsome arched bridge, approaching the mansion known as Ingfield, recently occupied by the Rev. Mr. Swale, ex-chaplain to the British Embassy at Paris. A large quantity of earth has been removed on the west side of the line nearly opposite the estate to fill up the embankments. The Settle Station ground has thus been raised to nearly the level of the rails, and makes a yard of considerable area—probably not less than ten acres. Within this space a commodious and well-built station has been erected, which has the further advantage of a convenient site in the town, instead of being, like the old one, more than a mile distant.

Significant earthworks were needed to build the embankments and cuttings, primarily through the physical exertions of the navvies. Tonnes of earth from the Anley cutting below Ingfield (now the Falcon Manor) were excavated and recycled to build the embankment through to Settle Station [1]. Beyond were two viaducts and more embankments, requiring a quarter of a million cubic yards of material. The disruption to the town lasted the best part of ten years as construction took place across the length of the line for the duration. By 1875 [WSA]:

- The road around Settle Junction has been diverted and improved with two bridges nearly finished "for the convenience of the landowners".
- The signal box at the new station has been erected and the station itself is being roofed-in and the Station Master's House foundations (and others) are ready for the superstructure.
- Six cottages (Cammock Lane) are being constructed and six at Salt Lake near Batty Green for the servants of the company and "are of a pretty order of architecture." "The erection of such structures shows a wise policy, as unless the men are comfortably housed, it will be a difficult task to keep them at their various posts, in the solitary and dreary places through which the line passes."

- New stations are to be built at the Craven Lime Kilns, Batty Green, Dent Head and Skipton.

- The Settle to Batty Green line is completed with the exception of sidings. Batty Moss (Ribblehead) Viaduct is practically finished and engines and trucks have been running over it for two months. The parapet walls are now being put on.

The railway opened for freight traffic in August 1875 and passenger trains began on 1st May 1876 although work continued for another two years. *"Settle presented, when we first saw it, a strange and confused appearance. The pretty passenger station, built of freestone and in Gothic style, was nearly finished; but around were whitewashed wooden sheds, the temporary offices or homes of the Company's staff and innumerable piles of contractors' materials no longer required, but ready marked off in lots for a great clearance sale."* [B]

The railway provided much-needed opportunities for working class labourers. Cornish mines were declining. Increasing mechanisation in agriculture and mills reduced the need for labour across the country. Workers went to local hiring markets or, if they could read, replied to newspaper adverts [4] which, in this case, emphasised good wages and lodgings. During the 1870s there were 28 different railway companies requiring workers so competition was stiff.

TUNNEL MINERS wanted at Blea Moor Tunnel, Settle and Carlisle Railway, No. 1 Contract. Wages, 6s. per day. Good lodgings immediately adjoining. Station, Ingleton *via* Leeds Parties of ten men will be passed down.—Apply Alfred Terry, Mid 1:nd Railway Offices, Settle

The Settle and Carlisle railway had a recruitment nightmare. Numerous navvies travelled here, took one look at the terrain and quickly went away again. This was a tough, physical job with experienced navvies expected to dig over 10 tonnes of material a day. It took up to a year to build the strength to do the job to receive full pay and this was just too much for some men.

Oh to be a navvy [F]

His first day as a navvy, he was home by 3 o'clock
His hands all cut and bloody, his face pale with the shock
He told me he had shifted 6 tonnes of earth that day
Only earned 2 shillings of the 5 that was his pay

Chorus: Oh to be a navvy, be a hard and drinking man
Oh to be a navvy, earn the best pay that he can
Oh to be a navvy, work the Settle Carlisle line
Oh to be a navvy, come the rain, the hail or shine

He grew up a strapping lad, he had worked his fathers land
With thoughts of easy money, he got more than he had planned
He thought he was a strong lad until he worked a navvies shift
Took him nigh on a full year, afore he could work the whole of it

His breakfast off a shovel, fried up by the gangers lad
2lbs of beef, a galleon of ale, on most days he will have
He's particular about his clothing, canvas shirt, red handkerchief
Moleskin trousers, square tailed coat, and a cudgel up his sleeve

Navvies often travelled around the country in gangs to work on contracted jobs. Navvy gangs had nicknames and clothing, such as neck ties and caps, to identify themselves *[C]*.

The work is carried on largely by the system of sub-contracting. One navvy undertakes to do a certain amount of work, and engages men under him, who look to him for payment; and by this means a man of ordinary experience and judgment is enabled to make a good living while the work lasts.

The spirit of clanism is very powerful among them—their antipathies and partialities being very strongly developed. Yet there is often a sub-stratum of good feeling and fellow-sympathy existing, which is not apparent to a superficial observer.

The delivery of letters by the postman in such a collection of huts is a task of surprising difficulty. Very few men are distinguished by their proper names. When first a man comes on to a 'job,' his fellows are on the look-out for some peculiarity, and if they detect one, they apply a name to it, by which its possessor is known for years, it may be. 'Lanky,' 'Gloucester,' 'Soldier,' 'Nobby,' 'Cuddy,' 'Caleb,' and scores of other names are given, so that it must have puzzled the census-taker to get a correct schedule of the denizens of these bleak moors.

Navvies needed to eat well to be strong enough to work and so their pay was a relatively high four shillings for a ten hour day. This was in the form of 'truck money' — tokens which could only be spent in the settlement stores, also run by the railway company. As their work was more dangerous, tunnellers were paid more than regular navvies at six shillings per day. Obviously, there was no sick pay or compensation for injury or death. Navvies generally lived hand to mouth, their *"only object is to exist, without casting a thought to the future"*, never mind thinking about the cost of a gravestone *[C]*.

The navvy can earn from three to four shillings a day, working ten hours; and if, by reason of the claims of a family, he works six days a week, can earn good wages; but, as a rule, he belongs to a spendthrift race, whose only object is to exist, without casting a thought to the future.

Some Settle navvies boarded with local families, generally in Upper Settle. However, being a small town hundreds of others lived in simple, temporary wooden 'navvy huts' close to their work sites. This hut *[ph1]*, originally in Appleby, was carefully restored and is now in the grounds of Settle Station water tower. It had been lime washed and had paper linings from a newspaper printed in 1878!

At the time of the 1871 census there were 5 'shanty towns' alongside the railway in Settle, but numbers would have varied over the seasons and years. There were 5 huts at Runley Bridge, 17 at Goldielands, 1 at Marshfield and 16 at Ashfield. The Ashfield settlement contained a 'hospital' of some sort and PC Alfred Phillipson lived at the Marshfield site. He would have been a busy man! There was a 'Tommy Shop' in a barn at the bottom of Duke Street run by the contracted supplier *Burgoin and Cocks* which provided 4000 loaves a day, plus the meat of four cows, fifteen sheep and pigs weekly. They even advertised in the Settle Almanac *[LSA]*. One journalist said, *"Their store is something like what we should expect in the backwoods of America. They appear to sell everything. They are butchers, bakers, hosiers, drapers — clothing the navvies and their families as well as feeding them"* [3].

Railway Provision & Clothing Stores.

Chief Depots—SETTLE & BATTY GREEN.

WHOLESOME PROVISIONS

Of every kind; great variety of

READY-MADE CLOTHES,

AND

BOOTS and SHOES, Good and Cheap.

Choice WINES and SPIRITS at the Settle Stores.

BURGOIN AND COCKS, Proprietors.

Moving up the valley there were 4 huts just south of Langcliffe, 4 at Oxgang (just below the site of the old Hoffmann Kiln), 21 at Stainforth and 15 at 'Elworth Bridge' — Helwith Bridge. There were over 1000 navvies and their families at Ribblehead and Blea Moor *[E]*. Life in Settle huts would have been far more comfortable than in those on the high exposed fells. Some navvies lived in Settle and travelled up to Ribblehead on workmen's trains.

A navvy village was not the ideal location for child rearing but some navvies had hardy wives who gave birth to children and brought them up in the huts. That's an interesting childhood! Typically, a navvy hut contained one such family who provided board and lodgings for a number of other, unmarried navvies, sometimes in shifts. One navvy hut wife was described as, *"A robust, powerful, purposeful dame, of immense energy, considerable surface roughness but real genuine kindliness of heart."* The family would have lived at one end of the hut, boarders at the other, with the central area for eating and cooking *[C]*.

In these cases, the contractors build a number of 'huts' of wood, covered with felt, tarred, and sometimes whitewashed; with a good, substantial cooking-range—a most essential consideration to a navvy's wife—in the centre of the hut; and partitioned-off sleeping-places at each end—one intended for the tenant and his wife, and the other for single-men lodgers. This latter is usually made so as to hold four pair of bed-stocks, each to accommodate two men; and where room is scarce, it is not an uncommon thing to find sixteen men lodging in one hut—eight in bed in the daytime, and eight at night; while the whole of the cooking depends on the wife of the tenant, who has her hands full in providing for such men and such appetites.

The residents of this hut recorded in the 1871 census return *(below)* are typical. The birthplaces of children describe the journey of George and Jane Gibbs around the country following work on new railways. Mortality for children of navvy families was even higher than usual as the gaps in child ages illustrate. Unsurprisingly most navvies and tunnellers were single men in their twenties and thirties. The navvies in this return came from far and wide. A noticeably high number of navvies gave false names — one man here called himself **Francis Frattlefarty** from Lichfield. One wonders about his personal hygiene? Unsurprisingly, he can't be traced any further. Several navvies had an unknown birthplace or name, recorded as 'NK' — not known.

Name	Relation	Condition	Age (M)	Age (F)	Occupation	Where Born
George Gibbs	Head	Mar.	32		Railway Miner	Gloucestersh: Gloucester
Frances Do	Wife.	Mar.		28		Cornwall: Towedreth
James H. Do.	Son		12			Do. Do
Lavinia Do.	Daur.			5		Derbysh: Vermwell
George Do	Son		3			Do: Do.
Mary Do	Daur			1		Yorksh: Stannaga
Francis Frullustarty	Boarder	Unm	27		Railway Labourer	Staffordsh: Lichfield
James Smith	Do	Unm	25		Do: Miner	Lancash: Liverpool
Richard Birley	Boarder	Unm	27		Railway Miner	Devonsh: Devonport
Thomas Watkins	Do.	Unm	26		Do: Do	Herefordsh: Clifford
Robert Rouse	Do	Unm	25		Do: Do	Suffolk: Thelnetham
James Thomas	Do	Unm	24		Do: D:	Devonsh: Plymouth

The navvy huts were serviced by a variety of tradesmen and professionals, such as Robert Ferris, brother of navvy **Thomas Ferris**, who travelled by horse and cart or on tradesmen's trains.

On New Year's Eve, 1875, the retail proprietors, Burgoin and Cocks, put on a supper for the railway workers of Contract No.1 at the Royal Oak in Settle where *Mrs Jane Batty* was *'the worthy hostess'*. Large though the Royal Oak is, the supper could only provide for a tiny fraction of the 2300 navvies who worked on this contract. During the evening several *"loyal toasts were proposed,"* and *"The evening was spent in a very convivial and agreeable manner"* [CH]. Perhaps there was a toast to those who were injured or had died during the building of the railway?

SETTLE.

SUPPER.—The employes on contract No. 1 of the new line of railway (Settle and Carlisle), were invited by the firm of Messrs. Burgoin and Cocks,—who have been connected with the Settle and Carlisle Railway since its commencement about six years ago, and who are now leaving the neighbourhood—to a supper at the the Royal Oak Hotel, on New Year's Eve. After doing ample justice to the good things provided for them by the worthy hostess, Mr. Burgoin was called to the chair, when the health of the Queen and other loyal toasts were proposed. The healths of Messrs. Burgoin and Cocks, the Midland Railway Company, the employes, and the hostess were drunk, interspersed with songs. The evening was spent in a very convivial and agreeable manner.

What do we know about the navvies who died?

These navvies were incredible men. 21st century portrayals of navvies evoke romantic notions of sterling achievement and understated heroism. The gritty reality was far more down to earth. 19th century working class life was a battle for survival to put food into mouths, punctuated by the death of loved ones and friends. When they signed (their mark) on the dotted line, did the navvies have any idea, or consider the risk to their health or lives? Probably not. It would have been irrelevant to them that the Settle and Carlisle railway would be regarded as one of the world's greatest in future centuries. It was just a job, but a really tough one. *"The spirit of the men who built this line is the best in England"* [D, J]

Richard Cartmell	23		John Owen	19
James Burkinsher	28		Robert Jackson	16
James Todd	21		Thomas Ferris	28
Henry Caswell	28		William Spencer	28
William Peacock	25		Thomas Smith	46
Joseph Smith	64		James Lashbrook	28
Joseph Uttley	41		Robert Ralph	41
Thomas Burton	36		James Smith	40
John Jones	17		Samuel Henry	25
Abraham Cooling	33		Thomas Cooper	23
William Potterton	29		John Barrett	53

Ribblehead Under Construction; Alan Fearnley

Navvy	Date of Death	Age at death	Occupation on death certificate	Cause of death on death certificate	Informant
Richard Cartmell	25 Feb 1871	23	Railway labourer	Continued Fever	Margaret Gifford, neighbour
James Burkinsher	20 May 1871	28	Railway labourer	Continued Fever	John Cook, railway worker
James Todd	25 Nov 1871	21	Tinner and brazier apprentice	Pthisis	Henry Todd, father
Henry Caswell	7 Mar 1872	28	Labourer	Injuries received from a wagon laden with earth accidentally passing over him on the new Settle and Carlisle Line	Thomas Parkinson Brown, deputy coroner
William Peacock	23 Apr 1872	25	Labourer	Accidentally killed by a crane falling and knocking him off a bridge into the River Ribble	Thomas Parkinson Brown, deputy coroner
Joseph Smith	9 May 1872	64	Railway labourer	Heart disease	Mark of Mary Ralph, landlady
Joseph Uttley	23 May 1872	41	Railway labourer	Heart disease	Alice Uttley, wife
Thomas Burton	18 Jun 1872	36	Labourer	Accidentally crushed and mortally wounded between two wagons, survived 3 days	Thomas Brown, coroner
John Jones	27 Jul 1872	17	Stoker on railway engine	Accidentally killed falling from a railway engine	Thomas Parkinson Brown, deputy coroner
Abraham Cooling	21 Aug 1872	33	Carpenter	Mortal injuries from a piece of timber accidentally falling upon his head, survived one hour	Thomas Brown, coroner
William Potterton	6 Dec 1872	29	Railway labourer	Compound fracture of right leg, pyaemia infection	Peter Day, railway labourer
John Griffith Owen	18 Feb 1873	19	Labourer	Accidentally killed by a crane falling and striking him	Thomas Parkinson Brown, deputy coroner
Robert Henry Jackson	25 Apr 1873	16	Son of James Jackson, stonemason, apprentice	Pthisis 4 months	James Jackson, father
Thomas Ferris	30 Apr 1873	28	Railway labourer	Inflammation of the lungs	Robert Ferris, brother
William Henry Spencer	7 Nov 1873	28	Smith and mechanic	Accidentally crushed between two wagons and killed	Thomas Brown, coroner
Thomas Smith, alias Bill Farrer	15 Mar 1874	46	Miner	Found dead in the River Ribble with no marks of violence upon his person	Thomas Parkinson Brown, deputy coroner
James Lashbrook	28 Mar 1874	28	Miner	Accidentally killed by explosion of a dynamite cartridge	Thomas Parkinson Brown, deputy coroner
Robert Ralph	24 May 1874	40	Stonemason	Pthisis, disease of the liver, dropsy	Mary Sewell, sister
James Harry Smith	22 Aug 1874	40	Railway labourer	Pthisis and pneumonia, acute, certified by Francis Green	Annie Smith, wife
Samuel Henry	15 Oct 1874	25	Stonemason	Pneumonia endocarditis	William Henry, brother
Thomas Cooper	22 Feb 1875	23	Railway labourer	Pneumonia Pthithis, 4 months, certified James Hartley	Hugh Cooper, brother
John Barrett	19 Apr 1875	53	Railway labourer	Liver disease 9 months	Mark of Elizabeth Thompson, neighbour

Railway workplace	Residence at death	Birth place	Father's occupation	Marital status	Gravestone
	died 'at Settle'	Whittingham, Preston	Weaver	Single	No
	died 'at Settle'	Mattersea, Nottinghamshire	Agricultural labourer	Single	No
	Townhead, Settle	Settle	Gardener	Single	Yes
No.1 cutting, Anley, Settle	died 'at Settle' at the hospital	Worcestershire	Shoemaker	Married, 1 son	No
Sherwood Brow, Stainforth	died 'at Settle' at the hospital	St Albans	Gardener	Single	No
Elworth Bridge	Settle	Preston	Unknown	Single	No
	Langcliffe, died 'at Settle' at the hospital	Coverdale	Farm labourer	Married, 3 children	No
Elworth Bridge No.7 cutting	died 'at Settle' at the hospital, Talbot Yard	Macclesfield	Unknown	Widowed	No
Batty Wife at Ribblehead	died 'at Settle' at the hospital	Wigan	Railway labourer	Single, assumed	Yes
	died 'at Settle'	Southwell, Nottinghamshire	Framework knitter	Married, 4 children	No
Runley Bridge	died 'at Settle', probably at the hospital	Sleaford Lincolnshire	Agricultural labourer	Single	No
No.3 cutting near Langcliffe	Langcliffe	Anglesey	Unknown	Single, assumed	Yes
	Bowskill's Yard, Settle	Bentham	Stonemason	Single	No
	died 'at Settle'	Newry	Unknown	Single	Yes
The new station ground in Settle	Twisleton's Yard	Settle	Smith and mechanic	Married, no children	Yes, Gigg
Stainforth	died 'at Settle'	Wakefield	Tailor	Married, 3 children	No
Tunnel near Ingleton	died 'at Settle'	Devon	Agricultural labourer	Single	No
	Bowskill's Yard, Settle	Settle	Joiner	Married, 3 children, wife also died	No
	died 'at Settle'	Leeds	Blacksmith	Married, 2 sons	No
	died 'at Settle'	Newry	Stonemason	Single	Yes
	died 'at Settle'	Newry	Stonemason	Single	Yes
	Poole's Yard, Settle	Somerset	Agricultural labourer	Married, no children	No

These men provided quite a research challenge! Several had common names or nicknames which were hard to trace especially as they moved around the country. Regional accent variations and made-up names resulted in inaccurate census returns. Unlike the middle classes, navvies were not in a position to place adverts for businesses, nor to feature in reports of local events. Typically, they would only be named in newspapers if they got into trouble with the law or died in a tragic accident. However, with the death certificates provided by FoSCL, church and local records, previous project findings, old OS maps, genealogical websites and 19th century newspapers we now know who most of our navvies were. We must not forget their wives about whom we know even less, sadly.

This was a diverse group of working class men with captivating stories to tell. They were the sons of labourers, agricultural labourers, weavers, framework knitters, tailors, butchers, blacksmiths, shoemakers and gardeners. Generally referred to as 'navvies', they had a range of jobs. The engineers had to work with the men who had been recruited. If the contractors at Ribblehead had more labourers and less stonemasons working for them, the viaduct may have had fewer arches and more embankments. 13 of the 22 navvies were 'railway labourers'. The 1871 census return for Settle records an influx of hundreds of 'railway labourers'. The number of stonemasons more than tripled from 19 in 1851 to over 65 in 1871. The number of blacksmiths more than doubled over that period too.

Occupation	Number
Railway labourer	13
Miner / tunneller	2
Engine stoker	1
Carpenter	1
Smith/mechanic	1
Stonemason	2
Apprentice	2

Three of our navvies were from Settle — the building of the railway was a welcome employment opportunity for the working classes. During the 1850s the Settle cotton mills had gone into decline and so numerous families had had to move to the Lancashire cotton mills, with Accrington being particularly popular. One navvy came from Bentham and another from Kettlewell. Further afield there were two navvies from Preston, two from Nottinghamshire and one from each of Wakefield, Leeds, Wigan, Macclesfield, Lincolnshire, St Albans, Worcestershire, Devon and Somerset. One was from Anglesey and three were from Newry, Ireland.

Year of death	Number
1870	0
1871	3
1872	8
1873	4
1874	5
1875	2

The statistics for the 12 months from March 1872 were shocking — nine of the deaths occurred, including six of the nine involving a coroner's inquest. These deaths took place across the whole of the line between Settle and Blea Moor at Ribblehead.

Eight navvies were married with children, one was widowed and 13 were single. The married men had an average of two children, with one man having four. The average age at death was 31.4 years, with the oldest being 64 and the youngest just 16. Over three-quarters of our navvies were aged 36 or under.

How did our navvies die?

Nine navvies died from tragic accidents which prompted coroners' inquests and one had a bad accident which, for some reason, didn't. The inquests revealed a catalogue of horrific injuries which even the most basic health and safety procedures may have prevented. 19th century newspapers didn't hold back with graphic details with little consideration for relations. For example, poor Thomas Cook was a railway platelayer in Carlisle. In 1875 he took his own life, *"ending my miserable existence"* whilst warning other men *"never to live with a mother-in-law"*! [5]

In our sample, the causes of death recorded by the coroner were:

Main cause of death	Number
Accidents	10
Infectious disease	9
Liver disease	1
Heart disease	2

A MATRIMONIAL CALAMITY.—Yesterday morning, a young man, 30 years of age, a platelayer on the Settle and Carlisle Railway, hanged himself on a post in a public drying-ground at Carlisle. Before doing so he wrote with a piece of chalk on a neighbouring wall the following message :—"I take the pleasure of riting these few lines, if it will be a warning to all young men never to live with a mother-in-law. Now I end my miserable existence."

- Accidentally killed by a crane falling and striking him

- Accidentally killed by a crane falling and knocking him off a bridge into the River Ribble

- Injuries received from a wagon laden with earth accidentally passing over him on the new Settle and Carlisle Line

- Accidentally crushed and mortally wounded between two wagons (2)

- Accidentally killed falling from a railway engine

- Mortal injuries from a piece of timber accidentally falling upon his head; survived one hour

- Accidentally killed by explosion of a dynamite cartridge. (In areas with more tunnels, the proportion of navvies killed by dynamite was significantly higher.)

- Found dead in the River Ribble with no marks of violence upon his person

In the last case **Thomas Smith** died after being seen *"the worse for liquor on Saturday night"*. Navvies **John Barrett** and **Robert Ralph** died with the longer term effects of alcohol, liver disease. So nearly 14% of our sample died of alcohol-related causes — a sobering thought!

Over half of our navvies died of disease. During the 19th century, infectious disease was just another of life's challenges and a third of all deaths were due to smallpox, typhoid, scarlet fever, measles, cholera, whooping cough or diphtheria. The smallpox vaccine was discovered as early as 1796 but effective treatment of other infections had to wait for a better understanding of germ theory and sanitation much later in the 19th century. Antibiotics were not in common use until 1940.

Nine of our navvies died of infectious disease; well above the national average. Navvy communities were a breeding ground for disease. Navvies couldn't afford to take time off for sickness and so travelled around the country harbouring germs, sharing them with others in their crowded navvy huts and workplaces. 'Social distancing' just didn't exist. In 1871 there was an outbreak of smallpox at the Ribblehead settlements killing 80 navvies, wives and children. This was not the direct result of intemperance as proposed by several cynics at the time, although the smallpox probably spread faster and further with the effects of alcohol. The clerk to the Settle Union, *John Lister,* asked the Midland Railway to contribute to the cost of 'Settle Smallpox and Fever Hospital' as it was thought that the outbreak was introduced by incoming navvies. The railway contributed £100.

Over half of the infections that killed our navvies were identified as some form of lung disease – tuberculosis, or pneumonia or both. Tuberculosis was also known as phthisis, consumption, scrofula and colloquially as 'the white plague', due to the pale skin of sufferers. It was a slow, progressive disease from which sufferers rarely recovered. Optimists said it allowed for a 'good death' as sufferers could arrange their affairs but it was a lengthy, agonising end of life. Two navvies died after unidentified 'continued fever'. Two others died of heart disease, no doubt exacerbated by the tough physical work conditions and their lifestyle. Medical provision was minimal, as young **John Jones** discovered.

The matching memorial plaques in the porches of Settle and Chapel-le-Dale churches are inscribed, *"To the memory of those who through accidents lost their lives in constructing the railway works between Settle and Dent Head. This tablet was erected at the joint expense of their fellow workmen and the Midland Railway Company 1869 to 1876."* Isn't it a shame the inscription didn't refer to those who died of disease too?

Where were the navvies buried?

The final resting place for most of these navvies was the 'Ancient' graveyard at Settle church with one in Giggleswick graveyard. At least six of the navvies died from accidents at their workplace along the line but were brought back to Settle for hospital treatment or for a coroner's inquest. Those suffering from diseases died in their lodgings with their family, landlady or fellow navvies 'present at death'.

The church sexton was responsible for maintaining the map of the graveyard to indicate where burials were located. Unfortunately, the sexton during these years was *William Perkin* who, despite written warnings from the church, didn't keep the map up to date so we will never know exactly where most of the navvies are buried. However, unusually, seven navvies had their lives commemorated with a gravestone. None of the 215 burials at Chapel-le-Dale have a gravestone. The navvy buried at Giggleswick church is with the rest of his family, commemorated with a gravestone.

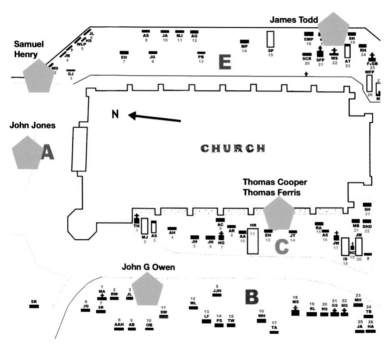

There was no specific pattern to burials in the graveyard so the navvies would have been buried in the next available plot. Many of the burials in the area to the north of the church were from working class families without gravestones so it wouldn't be surprising if some of our navvies were in there too. Sadly, the church has no knowledge of relations visiting any of the navvies' graves.

The lives of our navvies, by date of death; almost

Richard Cartmell, died 25th February 1871, physically exhausted

Richard was born in July 1847 in Goosnargh, a small village just north of Preston. He was the eldest of four children of **William Cartmell** and **Alice Sellers**, who made a living from 'power loom weaving' which had replaced the traditional hand loom weaving in the north-west of England.

Richard was tempted away to work on the railways as a labourer. Richard died on 25th February 1871, aged 23, of *'continued fever'* from which he had suffered for 18 days *[1]*. He had suffered from *'Purpera haemorragia'* for four days — these days this condition is only referred to in equine cases but is *"rupturing and slowly spreading blood under the skin brought about by too much exertion of muscles and the whole frame"*, which says much about the physical nature of the work of the navvy, even for a 23 year old man.

Twenty fifth February 1871 Settle	Richard Cartmell	Male	23 Years	Railway Labourer	Continued Fever 18 days Purpura Haemorragia 4 days contd	M. Gifford Present at the death Settle	

Richard's death was registered by 59 year old **Margaret Gifford**, widow of butcher *William Gifford*, who lived in the Shambles in Settle. Perhaps Richard had found accommodation in the centre of Settle, lodging with Margaret as a way of helping her make ends meet? Her son Harry had died of scarlet fever two years before.

Richard is buried in an unmarked grave somewhere in the Ancient Graveyard.

··· JC ···

James Burkinsher, died 20th May 1871, a victim of fever

James, born in 1843, was the son of an agricultural labourer, **William Burkinsher/Burkinshaw/Brukinshear** and his wife **Harriet Tumman**. They lived in Mattersea, which is technically in Nottinghamshire, but is just a few miles south of Doncaster. The Burkinsher family had lived in Mattersea for generations, farming small plots of land in the grounds of Mattersea Hall, *[ph2]* described in the 19th century as *"an excellent family residence"*! Navvies

could only dream of living somewhere like this! James' mother Harriet was unlucky in marriage. Her first husband, **George Simpson,** committed suicide just after their marriage. William was her second husband, who died, aged 60, after 20 years of marriage (when James was 13) and her third husband, **Matthew Doncaster,** died ten years after their marriage. Such was Victorian life — in the 19th century the average marriage lasted 14 years before the death of one spouse.

By the time of the 1861 census, James, along with many other Nottinghamshire men, worked as a miner, ideal experience for work as a railway tunneller. James does not appear on the 1871 census returns, just six weeks before his death, so may have been underground.

Twentieth May 1871 Settle	James Burkinsher	Male	28 years	Railway Labourer	Simple continued fever 1 month Certified	John Cook — In Attendance Settle

James died on 20th May 1871, aged 28, of *'continued fever'* from which he had suffered for a month. The person in attendance at his death was *John Cook*, a Settle carpenter on the railway who lived in Duke Street. John may have been a workmate or landlord (and also features as one of our 'winners and losers').

James is buried in an unmarked grave somewhere in the Ancient Graveyard.

James Todd, died 25th November 1871, a young apprentice

James worked as an apprentice tinner and brazier so his death may be connected to the railways. James was the sixth out of seven children of *Henry Todd [ph3]* and his wife **Sarah Harrison.** Sarah died at the birth of her next child, Robert, so James was brought up by Henry and elder siblings. Henry worked as the gardener for the Townhead estate in Settle for 53 years and lived in Townhead Cottage at the top of Castle Hill.

James died aged just 21, on 25th November 1871, of phthisis with his father present at the death.

Twenty fifth November 1871 Settle	James Todd	Male	31 years	Tinner and Brazier (apprentice)	Phthisis 1 year Certified	Henry Todd Present at the death Settle

James is buried with his parents in the graveyard. The grave is in the midst of those of the wealthy families who owned Townhead and who may well have paid for the stone.

In affectionate remembrance of Henry Todd, for 53 years the faithful servant and friend of the family at Townhead, Settle, died 25th March 1892 aged 85 years. Also of Sarah his wife died 1st May 1854, aged 44 years. And of James their son died 25th November 1871 aged 21 years

Henry Caswell, died 7th March 1872, run over by wagons

Henry, born in 1843 in Powick, near Malvern, was the seventh out of nine children of **William Caswell**, a shoemaker and his wife **Mary Anne Pride**. Mary Anne died when Henry was just six, after the birth of a daughter, Elizabeth, who also died a few weeks later. William and elder siblings brought up the family.

At the time of the 1861 census Henry was working as a labourer in Malvern. In 1867 he married **Mary Ann Whiting**, a labourer's daughter from Norfolk. They married in London and Henry described his occupation as an 'excavator', great for tunnelling on railways.

At the time of the 1871 census Henry and Mary Ann were living in Smethwick in the Black Country. Henry worked as a railway platelayer and they had an 11 month old son, **George Henry Caswell**. They were in Settle by March 1872. Henry died on 7th March 1872, aged 28, from *"injuries received from a waggon laden with earth accidentally passing over him on the new Settle and Carlisle Line"*.

Seventh March 1872 Settle	Henry Caswell	Male	28 years	Labourer	Died from injuries received from a waggon laden with earth accidentally passing over him on the new Settle and Carlisle Railway	Information received from Thos. P. Brown Deputy Coroner for Yorkshire Inquest held 8th March 1872

An inquest was held the following day. The report of the inquest avoided giving too many gruesome details as they had already been given in the previous issue *[1]*. That edition explained that Henry had been working at the No.1 cutting in Settle, at Anley. This cutting was particularly long and deep and tons of 'very hard grit' were excavated for use on other parts of the railway.

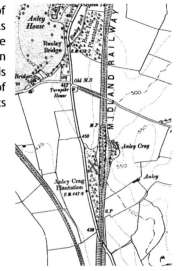

INQUEST.—An inquest was held on Saturday last at Settle, before Mr. Thomas P. Brown, deputy coroner, on the body of Henry Caswell, railway labourer, particulars of whose death was given in our last Saturday's issue. The jury returned a verdict to the effect that the deceased's death was caused from injuries received from a waggon laden with earth accidentally passing over him, on the new Settle and Carlisle Railway.

FATAL ACCIDENT.—A laborer employed in the construction of the Settle and Carlisle Railway whilst at work in the No. 1 Cutting, at Settle, on Thursday, was accidentally killed by four loaded waggons passing over him. As soon as the accident was discovered the man was conveyed to the hospital close by, where, on examination it was found his thigh was badly smashed, and it was deemed necessary to amputate the injured limb, which was accordingly done. The poor fellow did not, however, long survive the operation. Information has been given to the coroner, who, it is expected, will shortly hold an inquest.

John Birkbeck, the banker residing at Anley, was very concerned about his favourite bridge being destroyed to make the cutting and so it was taken down whilst he was called to attend a contrived 'emergency' at the bank. What would the navvies think of that?!

The paper reports "*As soon as the accident was discovered*", with no indication of how long that took, Henry was taken to the hospital close by and his thigh was amputated; he didn't survive the operation. Henry is buried in an unmarked grave in the Ancient graveyard.

By 1875 widow Mary Ann had moved to Wakefield and married **Henry Peaker,** a miner and they had at least four more children. In 1884 son George Henry Caswell, now aged 14, was baptised again, this time renamed '*George Robert Peaker son of Henry and Mary Ann Peaker*'. George was only two when his father Henry Caswell died, so would not have remembered him. George retained the name Peaker for the rest of his life and worked as a miner with a family of his own.

William Peacock, died 23rd April 1872, killed by a crane

William, born in 1846 in St Albans, was the fourth son of **James Peacock**, a gardener and his first wife, **Louisa Brown**, who died at the time of William's birth. William was brought up by his stepmother **Hannah Brown,** unrelated to Louisa. Two older brothers had died in infancy.

William, now a labourer, had arrived in Settle by 1872. He died on 23rd April 1872, aged 25, "*Accidentally killed by a crane falling on him and knocking him off a bridge into the River Ribble*".

Twenty third April 1872 Settle	William Peacock	Male	25 years	Labourer	Accidentally killed by a Crane falling and knocking him off a Bridge into the River Ribble	Information received from Thomas Parkinson Brown, Deputy Coroner for Yorkshire Inquest held 25 April 1872

The coroner's inquest *[4]* explained that William was working with others at Sherwood Brow, near Stainforth, lowering some timber with a crane at the bridge. This section of the railway had been an engineering challenge. The course of the river had to be diverted and two large bridges built over the river, both at acute angles. As the chains around the timber were loosened, the crane overturned and fell into the River Ribble, taking William with it. William was the only unlucky casualty. Incredibly, in this case, there were no recommendations about health and safety. William is buried in an unmarked grave in the Ancient graveyard.

An accident, which terminated fatally to a man named William Peacock, employed on the new Settle and Carlisle Railway, happened on Tuesday. The deceased, along with others, was on the bridge at Sherwood Brow, near Stainforth, engaged in lowering some timber. Whilst the chain was being loosed from the timber the crane overturned and fell into the river below, taking with it the man Peacock and another. The rest of the men succeeded in getting clear of the crane before it fell. Peacock was found much crushed, and was at once conveyed to the hospital, where he died the same night. The other man was not much injured. Deceased was 25 years of age, and a native of St. Albans.

·· JT ···

Joseph Smith, died 9th May 1872 after an argument

Joseph, born in 1808, was a single man from Preston. At the time of the 1871 census, he worked as a railway labourer, lodging in one of the 15 navvy huts at 'Elworth Bridge'. There were four railway workers in the *'Wood Hut'*, lodging with the family of Christopher Knowles, a stone-waller from Malham.

22

Labouring on the railway was a tough physical job and so most navvies were in their twenties or thirties. Joseph must have been a strong man, or desperate. He died on 9th May 1872, aged 64, from heart disease in 'Settle'.

Ninth May 1872 Settle	Joseph Smith	Male	64 Years	Railway labourer	Heart disease certified	+ the mark of Mary Ralph Present at the death Settle

It would not be surprising for a navvy aged 64 to have heart problems but perhaps something else contributed to Joseph's attack? On the 21st March Joseph went to the Golden Lion Inn at Horton in Ribblesdale just a couple of miles up the valley. Joseph separated a fight between fellow navvy **John Smith** (no relation), and 'Harry the carpenter'. During the scuffle John Smith stole £15 in silver from Joseph. There was a local hearing on the case. The newspaper report suggests that, in a swift sleight of the hand, John took the money from Joseph's waistcoat whilst commenting on his buttons and then fled with the proceeds to Batty Green [1].

INGLETON.

ROBBERY.—John Smith, a navvy, was brought up under remand, before the Rev. Richard Denny, at the Court House, on the 28th ult., and charged with robbing Joseph Smith, on the 21st ult., at the Golden Lion Inn, Horton-in-Ribblesdale, of 15 sovereigns. The facts of the case were these : Joseph Smith, of Helwith Bridge, laborer, went to the Golden Lion on the 20th ult. rather fresh, between 7 and 8 o'clock p.m. He gave to Mr. Hazledon, the landlord, 16 sovereigns to take care of for him. Next morning he requested that £1 might be returned to him in silver, and in the afternoon he desired that the remainder, viz., £15, might be returned to him, and this was done. After this, it appears that a quarrel arose between John Smith, and Harry, the carpenter, and that the said Joseph Smith stood between them to prevent a fight. John Smith then remarked that the buttons of Joseph Smith's waistcoat were off, and that he (Joseph Smith) pulled open the said waistcoat, and immediately left the house. Joseph Smith then, on examining his pocket, found that his money was gone. The prisoner was traced to the house of Thomas Pearson, innkeeper, Horton, when, after spending between three and four pounds in clothes, &c., he asked Mrs. Pearson to save 10s. for him. She, however, returned it to him at his request the same evening. He remained there all night, but left next morning. P.C. Walker having received information of the robbery, went in pursuit of the prisoner, and found him at Batty Green, and charged him with the robbery. The hearing was long and tedious, the result being that the prisoner was committed to the sessions for trial.

The hearing was *"long and tedious"* and John Smith was committed for trial. Unfortunately, Joseph died just six weeks later and there are no further reports about the case. Perhaps John got away with it?

Mary Ralph was present at Joseph's death. Mary (Lord) Ralph was the wife of *William Ralph*, a successful quarry owner and blue flag merchant *[LSA]*. Whilst William was running that business, wife Mary ran a 'common lodging house' business in part of their large property in Victoria Street in Upper Settle. Lodging houses provided cheap accommodation for working class people, just one step up from the workhouse. They were cramped and generally unpleasant with a poor reputation as a hotbed of crime, disease and prostitution. 'Guests' paid a few pence for their accommodation on a daily basis and were expected to leave the property during the day to encourage them to work.

If Joseph had been unwell and unable to work on the railway it is likely that he would have left the navvy hut and returned to cheaper accommodation in Settle, which would explain why landlady Mary registered his death *[1]*.

Joseph is buried in an unmarked grave in the Ancient graveyard.

··· JՐ ···

Joseph Uttley, died 23rd May 1872 from a heart attack

Joseph was born in 1830 in Coverdale, near Kettlewell, in the Yorkshire Dales. His father, **John Uttley**, was a farm labourer and Joseph followed his lead. In Settle, in 1866, Joseph married **Alice Bentham** from Arncliffe, who had worked as a servant in the Queen's Arms Inn in Littondale. They moved to Langcliffe, near Settle, where they had three children. By the time of the 1871 census Joseph was employed as a railway labourer and they lived in Twisleton's Yard in Upper Settle. One of their neighbours was **William Henry Spencer**, fellow navvy, who also died whilst doing his job on the railway.

| Twenty third May 1872 Settle | Joseph Uttley | Male | 41 years | Railway labourer | Heart disease certified | Alice Uttley In Attendance Langcliffe |

Joseph died of heart disease on 23rd May 1872, aged 41 and Alice was with him when he died. By then they were living back in Langcliffe. Joseph probably spent his last days in hospital in Settle and so was buried in an unmarked grave in Settle graveyard rather than at Langcliffe.

Alice was a fertile woman. Before she married Joseph, she had given birth to two sons **Miles** and **John** who lived with the Uttley family once Alice had married Joseph. Alice had Miles when she was just 17. Some 15 months after Joseph had died, Alice had another child, **Isabella**. By 1877, Alice had moved to Barnoldswick where she married widow **Richard Slater**, a carter and had another two daughters. All the children stayed in Barnoldswick establishing their own families and working in the mills. This is the family of Joseph and Alice's son **Thomas Uttley** *[ph4]*, a cotton weaver, third from the right on the back row.

··· ☞ ···

Thomas Burton, died 18th June 1872, crushed between wagons

At the time of the 1871 census Thomas, from Macclesfield, Cheshire, lived in Settle at Talbot Yard behind the Talbot Inn. He was widowed and worked as a carpenter. We do not know much more about his background.

Thomas died on 18th June 1872, aged 36. The inquest into his particularly unpleasant death decided that he was *"Accidentally crushed and mortally injured between two waggons, survived 3 days."*

The inquest was held one day later at the Commercial Hotel in Commercial Yard in Settle. Thomas was an employee of the *'new Settle and Carlisle railway'* working at No.7 cutting at 'Elworth Bridge'. Even the inn was known as the 'Elworth Bridge Inn' in those days. When the railway was built, the council had refused permission for a level crossing over the road at Helwith Bridge, so the Midland Railway had to re-route the river and completely rebuild the bridge (as a substantial arched viaduct), to allow room for both the railway and river underneath.

FATAL ACCIDENT.—An accident happened on Saturday last, to a man named Thomas Burton, an employee on the new Settle and Carlisle Cailway. The accident occurred at number seven cutting at Elworth Bridge, near to Settle. It appeared Burton had got behind some earth wagons to protect himself whilst a blast was being let off, and about the same time an engine with wagons attached came up, and before the poor fellow was aware of his dangerous position, he was jammed between the wagons and sadly crushed. He was immediately conveyed to the Hospital, but with very little hope that he would survive, he lingered, however, until Tuesday last, when he died. An inquest was held on Wednesday at the Commercial Hotel, Settle, before Mr Brown, coroner, when a verdict to the effect that the deceased accidentally met with his death under the above circumstances was returned. The jury, sitting in the above inquest resolved to send the following recommendation to the directors of the Midland Railway Company :—"The body of Thomas Burton, 26 hours after death being in an advanced state of decomposition, the effluvia offensive and sickening to the jury, cannot but be detrimental to the health of the patients confined in the Hospital, and to the Master and matron of the establishment, and during the hot weather is likely to be a prolific source of disease in the locality ; and the jury therefore urgently recommend the erection of a dead house detached from the Hospital as a means of remedying the present unsatisfactory state of things

Thomas hid behind some wagons to protect himself when a blast went off, unaware that a train was approaching and so was crushed between the wagons. He survived for three agonising days [4].

In a telling insight into the conditions, medical procedure and health and safety measures of 1872, the report concluded; *"The body of Thomas Burton, 26 hours after death being in an advanced state of decomposition, the effluvia offensive and sickening to the jury, cannot but be detrimental to the health of the patients* confined in the Hospital, and the master and matron of the establishment, and during the hot weather is likely to be a prolific source of disease in the locality; and the jury therefore urgently recommended the erection of a dead house detached from the hospital as a means of remedying the present unsatisfactory state of things". Medical Officer **Edwin Septimus Green** successfully applied for the dead house and a washhouse.

Thomas is buried in an unmarked grave somewhere in the Ancient Graveyard.

··J┌···

John Jones, died 27th July 1872, a young stoker

John, born in 1855, was the eldest of four children of **John** and **Sarah Jones**. John and Sarah started their family in Wigan but at the time of the 1871 census were living in a navvy hut at Langcliffe with the three youngest children and five lodging railway labourers. John (Snr) and 13 year old brother Thomas were also working as railway labourers. Perhaps John (Jnr) was working a shift somewhere at the time?

A couple of months later, lodger and labourer **William Turner**, was taken to court for stealing John's slop jacket, a billycock hat, a bible and a pocket handkerchief.

THEFT BY A LODGER.—William Turner, a railway labourer, who, previous to his apprehension, lodged at the house of John Jones, also a railway labourer, at Langcliffe, was brought up in custody on Saturday last, before the Rev. H. J. Swale, and C. Ingleby, Esqrs., charged with stealing a slop jacket, billycock hat, bible, and a pocket handkerchief, the property of John Jones. The prisoner left his lodgings early on Saturday morning, and shortly afterwards the articles, before enumerated, were missed. Information was given to the police, and the prisoner was apprehended by P.C. Phillipson on the same morning near to "Cleatop Cutting" with the whole of the missing property in his possession. The prisoner pleaded guilty, and was committed to prison for one month with hard labour.

It's interesting that a navvy family such as the Jones' was sufficiently God-fearing to carry a bible in their luggage around the country. William left the lodging in the morning and was arrested with the stolen items near Cleatop Cutting on the other side of Settle. William pleaded guilty and was imprisoned for a month with hard labour[1]

Twenty seventh July 1872 Settle	John Jones	Male	17 years	Stoker on a Railway Engine	Accidentally killed by falling from a Railway Engine	Information received from Thomas Parkinson Brown, Deputy Coroner for Yorkshire Inquest held 29 July 1872

John (Jnr) died when he was just 17. He had been working as an engine stoker at Batty Wife, Ribblehead, feeding coal into the engine. He died on 27th July 1872, after falling off his engine and injuring his arm and thigh [1].

INQUEST. – An inquest was held on Monday last, at the Commercial Hotel, before Mr. J, P. Brown, Deputy Coroner, respecting the death of John Jones, a young man, aged 17 years, who at the time of the accident was employed as a stoker, at Batty Wife, near Ingleton, on the new Settle and Carlisle Railway. The deceased met with his accident on Saturday last. Whilst in the act of doing something in connection with his engine he fell off, coming in contact with the abutment on the side, causing injuries to his arm and thigh. He was conveyed the same night to the hospital at Settle, but died shortly afterwards. The jury returned a verdict that the deceased was accidentally killed by falling from a railway engine.

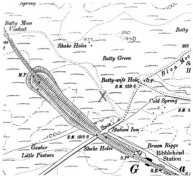

An inquest was held into John's death, at the Commercial Hotel in Settle, with a verdict of *"accidentally killed by falling from a railway engine"* [1]. *"He was conveyed the same night to the hospital in Settle"* which is a bumpy 12 mile trek even today, never mind with broken bones and no pain relief. Comfort would have been minimal in the 'ambulance' — a covered horse-drawn cart.

In memory of John Jones of Ingleton Fells who died on the 27th of July 1872, Aged 17 years. "Affliction seized my dear son and snatched him from my sight, but Jesus took him to his breast and claimed him as his right"

John's poor mother obviously arranged for the inscription on the gravestone. At the time of subsequent census returns John (Snr) worked as an innkeeper in Hull and then as a farmer at Wrightington, north of Wigan with Sarah and the other children.

Abraham Cooling, died 21st August 1872, a carpenter killed by a piece of timber

Abraham was born in 1841 in Southwell, Nottinghamshire, the youngest of eight children of **George Cooling** and **Elizabeth Blatts**. George Cooling was a framework knitter, producing hosiery and lace which were sold across the country. Abraham began his working life as an agricultural labourer in Winkburn, not too far from home. In 1863 he married **Sarah Sellers** (no relation to navvy Richard Cartmell's mother) from Tideswell in Derbyshire. By the time of the 1871 census they lived in Mansfield with three young children. Abraham worked as carpenter, well skilled for railway work.

Within the year the family had moved to Settle. Abraham died on 21st August 1872, aged 33, with *"mortal injuries from a piece of timber accidentally falling upon his head"* [1]. Abraham survived one hour.

> **SETTLE.**
> Fatal Accident.—Abraham Colling, a carpenter employed on the new Settle and Carlisle Railway, was accidentally killed on the 21st instant by a piece of timber falling upon his head. An inquest was held on the 23d inst. before Mr. T. Brown, coroner, when a verdict of "Accidental death" was returned.

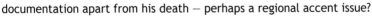

Sarah gave birth to a daughter **Mary Jane** who was baptised in Settle on 1st September 1872, *'father deceased'*. Did Abraham ever see his daughter? Did Abraham's death prompt Mary Jane's arrival? We shall never know. Abraham was buried in an unmarked grave.

Sarah took her four children to Oldham where they remained for the rest of their lives. Youngest daughter Mary Jane married **Samuel Bottomly Worrell**, a labourer, but died soon afterwards, presumably due to childbirth complications. Abraham and his family were named 'Cooling' on all documentation apart from his death — perhaps a regional accent issue?

···JՐ···

William Potterton, died 6th December 1872 with an infected broken leg

William was born in 1843 in Timberland, a small market town in rural Lincolnshire. He was the third of eight children of **Frank Potterton** and **Mary Green**. Lincolnshire was a county of agricultural labourers and market gardeners, with Frank included. William's brothers all became agricultural labourers in Lincolnshire and his sisters married agricultural labourers in Lincolnshire. For some reason, William decided to work on the railways.

William died on 6th December 1872, aged 29, in 'Settle' suffering from *'pyaemia'* after a compound fracture of the right leg. Pyaemia is a type of sepsis infection causing abscesses and, in the days before antibiotics, was almost always fatal. Despite a compound fracture of William's right leg, there was no inquest into his death.

Sixth December 1872 Settle	William Patterton	Male	29 years	Railway Labourer	Compound fracture of right leg Pyaemia certified	X The Mark of Peter Day Present at the death Settle

William's death was registered by **Peter Day,** another railway labourer. Peter and his wife **Lucy Randall** were from Cambridgeshire but spent their lives moving around the country to work. Peter had previously worked in Barnsley as an 'excavator'. At the time of the 1871 census Peter and Lucy lived in one of the five navvy huts at Runley Bridge looking after six other railway labourers. It's likely that William boarded with Peter or worked in the same gang as him.

William is buried in an unmarked grave somewhere in the Ancient graveyard.

·· ⨎ ···

John Griffith Owen, died 18th February 1873, a talented singer killed by a crane

It would be hard to find a Welsh name more common than John Owen, especially on the island of Anglesey and so it's impossible to trace this man's roots. However, he is the best known of Settle's navvy fatalities.

John G Owen's gravestone tells us that he was born in 1854 and was from Holyhead on Anglesey. There were nine John Owens registered on Anglesey in 1853/4. Four have mother's maiden name of Jones, two of Owen and also a Roberts, Evans and Williams. It really was a common name. At the time of the 1871 census, a John Owen from Holyhead, born in 1854, was lodging with his father John and brother Henry in *'No.9 railway hut'* at Crosby Garrett near Kirkby Stephen, all working as *'quarryman and miner'*. This could be the same John.

Sacred to the memory of John G Owen of Holyhead who died at Settle Feby 18th 1873 aged 19 years. Ai mewn bedd man loan back -O l'e. loan sy'n llwch bellach. Ond daw'n ol etto'n iach At ail vesi'n hi tlysach.
(Young John is now in his grave, John that is all ashes now, But he'll come back a second time, A thousand times better)

John settled into and contributed to Settle life. In November 1872, John performed for the Temperance Lifeboat Crew Society to raise funds for a lifeboat [1]. Incredibly, despite being some 35 miles from the nearest coast, Settle folk raised enough money to build and launch six lifeboats between 1868 and 1912, saving 148 lives in all. They were even paraded through the streets of Settle! Three boats were stationed in Anglesey so John's contribution was most apt.

SETTLE.

TEMPERANCE LIFE BOAT CREW —The members and friends of the above society gave the first of their en-entertainments this season on Saturday evening last. Captain Phillipson in the chair. The Hall was well filled with a very enthusiastic audience. The programme, which comprised songs, readings, recitations, and dialogues, was gone through in a very creditable manner. The reading in the Lancashire dialect by Master R. Lambert, entitled "Owd Shunt" kept the audience convulsed with laughter, and was deservedly applauded. The dialogues with the assistance of a few friends were very creditably rendered. Mr. John Owen very efficiently sung a Welsh song.

John died three months later on 18th February 1873, aged 19, *"Accidentally killed by a crane falling and striking him".*

Eighteenth February 1873 Langcliffe	John Owen	male	19 years	Labourer	Accidentally killed by a Crane falling and striking him	Information received from Thos Parkinson Brown Deputy Coroner for Yorkshire. Inquest held 18th February 1873

SETTLE—FATAL ACCIDENT.—John Owen, aged nineteen years, whilst working underneath a crane in No. 3 cutting, near Langcliffe, on the new Settle and Carlisle Railway, was killed on Tuesday last by one of the legs or supports of the crane falling upon him, causing his instant death. An inquest was held the same evening, when a verdict of " Accidentally killed " was returned by the jury, who recommended that for the future all the cranes used on the line should undergo an inspection daily by some competent person in the employ of the Midland Railway Company.

The report of the inquest describes that he was working underneath a crane in No.3 cutting near Langcliffe when one of the crane supports fell on him, killing him instantly [2]. In this case the jury actually recognised the need for better Health and Safety measures. They recommended, *"That for the future all the cranes used on the line should undergo an inspection daily by some competent person in the employ of the Midland Railway Company."* Now that's a good idea.

John is buried in Settle graveyard and has a fine stone, thought to be arranged by fellow navvies. One source says *"Owen's sorrowing mates attended the funeral at Settle Parish Church."* John was working and died at Langcliffe, but his body would have been brought to Settle for the coroner's inquest which may explain why he was buried at Settle rather than Langcliffe.

Tom Twisleton, a local poet, was captivated by John's tragic story and wrote a poem of some 15 verses. This was Tom Twisleton's only 'non dialect' poem. John was obviously a well respected and popular young man. Being in the Victorian era, the second half of the poem suggests ways to view his death as a matter of fact and inevitability. Of course, his passing should be rejoiced.

No farewells spoken
As he went forth at dawning of day
For little they thought, ere the morning had fled,
That the summons would call him away.

His face was
bright as morning spring
His heart free from sorrow and shame
And blythe as a lark, he would carol and sing
Hymns, in praise of his maker's name.

As oft 'twas his custom, whilst plying his toil
To enliven his task with a song
Or, with friends interchanging the joke or the smile,
To make labour pass lightly along.

He hath greeted his mates at the cutting of rock
And to work they have gone with a will.
Whilst he, humming a tune, kept time to the stroke
Of the rattling hammer and drill

The crane groaned and creaked and loud roared the shot
And the whistling engine went by them

These were every day things and they heeded them not
Nor dreamed they that danger was nigh them

But hark! a strange sound for a moment is heard
The crane that overhangs them is broken
And the heavy jib falls ere a hand can be stirred
Or a sentence of warning be spoken

In a breath, in an instant, it falls down the rock
And the workmen are scattered below
But all, except one, have escaped from the shock
He, alone, have received the fell blow.

They raise him up gently and utter his name
Tis in vain — he hath breathed his last breath
The spirit hath fled unto Him, whence it came
And the body is silent in death.

Ah! now heavy sobs convulse the strong breast
And tears trickle down the hard face
As they take the remains of the fairest and best
And bear them away from the place

Oh man in thy power! Oh youth in thy pride!
trust not in thy strength or thy skill.
When the messenger calls thee to lay them aside
Be prepared to submit to his will.

But how often it happens, that we of short sight,
Are apt to lament or complain
When death takes the hopeful, the young and the bright
While the wretch lingers on in his pain.

But thou, whose we are and whose the world is,
Thou, who wash'd out our sins with Thy blood
In Thy goodness and wisdom does nothing amiss
But arranges all things for our good.

Look thou down, in Thy mercy and pitying power
on the parents who mourn for their son
Give them strength to look up in affliction's dark hour
And say, 'Let the Lord's will be done'.

Thou his sun has gone down, ere it reach'd the noonday
Though sudden and fearful the blow
Yet pause and reflect — he hath but gone the way
We all, sooner or later, must go.

Then dry up the tear, and let sorrowing cease
When the body is laid neath the sod;
For, rejoicing above at its early release
The spirit is present with God.

···JⲄ···

Robert Henry Jackson, died 25ᵗʰ April 1873, our youngest casualty

Robert Henry, born in 1857 in Bentham, was the son of **James Jackson**, a stone mason from Preston and his wife **Ann Bibby**. The family moved to Settle in 1860 and lived in the Bowskills Yard cottages. Ann had four sons and a daughter before she died in 1865; she is buried in the graveyard with two infant children, **Margaret Ann** and **William Edward Jackson**. James then married **Margaret Bleazard** who helped to bring up the remaining children.

At the time of the 1871 census Robert Henry, aged 14, was apprenticed to a blacksmith, possibly William or Johnny Bowskill who lived next door. Stonemason and navvy **Robert Ralph**, who died the following year, was also a neighbour. Robert Henry died on 25ᵗʰ April 1873, after four months of phthisis and his father was present at his death. Unhelpfully, the death records his occupation as *"son of James Jackson, stonemason"*. As apprenticeships tended to take seven years, typically from the ages 14-21, he was probably still working as a blacksmith's apprentice. Robert Henry's death was registered by his father.

Twenty fifth April 1873 Settle	Robert Henry Jackson	male	16 years	Son of James Jackson Stonemason	Phthisis 4 months Certified	James Jackson Present at the death — Settle

Robert is buried in an unmarked grave somewhere in the Ancient graveyard, hopefully with his mother and the two siblings. After the railway had been built the rest of the family moved to Lancaster.

···JⲄ···

William Henry Spencer, died 7th November 1873, crushed between wagons

William Henry Spencer, born in 1845, was the son of **William Spencer**, one of the prolific family of plasterers and slaters in Settle, and his wife **Frances Procter**, living in Upper Settle close to the old Primitive Methodists' Chapel.

William Henry undertook an apprenticeship in mechanics and, at the time of the 1871 census, was described as a 'smith and mechanic' living in Twisleton's Yard with his wife. His neighbour was **Joseph Uttley,** fellow navvy, who also died during the building of the railway. In 1867 William Henry had married **Martha Cook**, a rope maker's daughter from Liverpool, who was nearly ten years his senior.

On 7th November 1873, aged 28, William Henry was working in the *'new station ground'* in Settle when he met his death. He was described as a *'fireman on a railway engine.'*

Seventh November 1873 Settle	William Henry Spencer	Male	28 years	Fireman on a Railway Engine	Accidentally Crushed between two Waggons and Killed	Information received from Thomas P. Brown Deputy Coroner for Yorkshire Inquest held 8 November 1873	Fifteenth November 1873

The coroner's inquest at the Commercial Hotel explained *"Whilst engaged in his ordinary occupation he by some means got between the buffers of some waggons and was severely crushed"* [1].

FATAL ACCIDENT.—An accident, which terminated fatally, happened on Friday last to a young man, named William Henry Spencer, a resident of Settle, and employed on the new Station ground of the Settle and Carlisle Railway. Whilst engaged in his ordinary occupation he by some means got between the buffers of some of the waggons and was severely crushed. He was conveyed to his home, but only survived few hours. An inquest was held on the following evening at the Commercial Hotel, by Mr. Brown, the coroner, when a verdict of " Accidental death" was returned.

Despite living in Settle, William Henry was buried in Giggleswick. Why? William Henry was one of nine siblings. Tragically, seven of those siblings had died in infancy. The first of two of them, Richard and Anthony died before the graveyard at Holy Ascension church was opened and so were buried in Giggleswick. Naturally William and the remaining siblings were buried with them. Their gravestone is huge and stands alone behind the altar of the church.

To the memory of the following children of William Spencer of Settle and Frances his wife:
Richard Spencer died 6th Feb'y 1837 aged 6 months
Anthony Spencer died 24th May 1838 aged 3 weeks
Henry Spencer died 19th May 1841 aged 9 years

William Spencer died 25th Sep'r 1841 aged 4 weeks
Agnes Spencer died 26th Dec'r 1847 aged 4 years
Albert Spencer died 16th March 1848 aged 19 weeks
Mary Ann Spencer died 26th Dec'r 1854 aged 15 years

Thou art gone to the grave but we will not deplore thee, Whose God was thy ransom, thy guardian and guide. He gave thee and took thee, and he will restore thee, And death has no sting, for the Saviour hath died.

Frances Spencer mother to the above died 12th Dec'r 1861 aged 50 years.
William Henry Spencer died Nov'r 7th 1873 aged 28 years.
Also of the above William Spencer of Settle who died July 14th 1884 aged 73 years.

William Henry's widow, Martha, presumably remarried. William Henry's mother Frances had died when he was 16. His father William lived with the only surviving child **Nancy**, who had married **John Ball**, a quarry labourer. Nancy ran one of the common lodging houses on Albert Hill in Settle whilst bringing up seven sons and a daughter. Her family had its own share of tragedy. Their 16 year old son, **Mark William Ball**, worked on the railway at Batty Green at Ribblehead. In April 1877 he took his own life whilst running an errand for his foreman.

Mark William's disappearance was not noticed that day. His father, John, supposed he had missed the workmen's train back to Settle and stayed over with someone. Obviously, there were no phones! Mark was discovered by workmen early the following morning *[CH]*. John, Nancy, son Mark William and an infant daughter **Florence May** are buried in an unmarked grave in Giggleswick churchyard.

William (Snr) died in 1884, aged 71, having spent his last years in the workhouse infirmary which was the only medical provision available for the poor. He must have been heartbroken. This was such an unlucky family.

SUICIDE AT BATTY GREEN.—On Thursday, the 24th ult., a youth named Mark William Ball, who resided with his parents at Settle, and was employed on the railway at Batty Green, committed suicide on the above day. It appears that he was sent an errand by the foreman of the works to a small cabin a short distance from Batty Green. As the foreman was attending a funeral on the afternoon of that day, the boy's absence was not noticed. About ten minutes past six o'clock on Friday morning two workmen entered the cabin, and there found the boy suspended by the neck with a handkerchief, quite dead. The men left him, and the body was not cut down until the arrival of P. C. Brown, from Ingleton, at a quarter to ten o'clock. The boy's father found him missing on Thursday evening, on the arrival of the workmen's train at Settle, but thought he had stopped all night with some one. An inquest was held at the Railway Tavern, Batty Green, on Monday, before T. P. Brown, Esq., and a verdict returned that he had committed suicide, but there was no evidence to show the state of his mind. Deceased was 16 years of age. The Coroner remarked in his address that it was the duty of the parties who first found him to have cut him down.

Thomas Smith, (alias Bill Farrer), died 15th March 1874, the worse for liquor

Thomas was born in 1831 in Wakefield, one of five children of a tailor, **William Smith,** and his wife **Elizabeth Brook.** Thomas married **Eliza Seal,** the daughter of **Samuel Seal** who ran a quarry near Wakefield. Eliza's brothers, **Stephen, James** and **Walter** continued their father's business and were employers of numerous men, women and children. They specialised in cutting scythe stones so were 'scythestone cutters'. Initially Thomas worked as a plasterer in South Yorkshire while Eliza brought up two sons and a daughter. Another daughter died in infancy. By 1874 Thomas and the family were in Stainforth where Thomas had found work on the railway as a miner (tunneller).

On 15th March 1874, aged 43, Thomas was *'found dead'* in the River Ribble near to King's Mill.

SETTLE.

MAN DROWNED.—On Sunday last the body of a man was seen in the river Ribble near to King's Mill, Settle, and on its being got out of the water, it was identified as the body of Thomas Smith *alias* Bill Farrer, who had been employed on the new line of railway here. The body was conveyed to the Royal Oak Inn, where an inquest was held on Tuesday last, before Thomas P. Brown, Esq, deputy coroner, when evidence was given that deceased was seen the worse for liquor late on Saturday night, going in the direction of Giggleswick, and it is supposed he had mistaken the road, and wandered down to the river side, and accidentally fallen in. There were no marks of violence found on his body, and the jury returned a verdict of "Found dead." The deceased was 43 years of age, and resided at Stainforth.

There is no indication how long he had been there, nor when he actually died. The coroner said there were *"no marks of violence on his person"* implying that he was not assaulted. This inquest took place at the Royal Oak Inn. The newspaper report said that Thomas seemed to have fallen in the river near King's Mill being *"the worse for liquor late on Saturday night"*[1]. When Thomas decided to work as a navvy, he probably didn't consider 'drowning in the Ribble' as a likely danger of the job.

The paper also tells us he resided at Stainforth, perhaps at one of the navvy huts there. Like many other navvies, Thomas had an alias, 'Bill Farrer', which was probably linked to his gang of railway workers. The Farrer family owned the Clapham estate — perhaps Thomas resembled one of them? Thomas is buried in an unmarked grave in the Ancient graveyard.

Eliza took the three children back to Wakefield. Their sons found employment in her family's scythestone cutting business and their daughter married a man who was also employed there. Eliza died, in October 1896, in Ackworth near Wakefield, just six months after their son, Walter.

···ᒍᚱ···

James Lashbrook, died 28th March 1874, blown up by dynamite

James, born in 1846 in Westleigh near Barnstable, Devon was the second of five children of **William Lashbrook**, an agricultural labourer and his wife **Mary Ann Lock**. James chose to work as a miner, a common occupation in the south-west and good preparation for railway tunnelling.

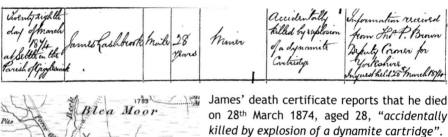

James' death certificate reports that he died on 28th March 1874, aged 28, *"accidentally killed by explosion of a dynamite cartridge"*.

A MAN KILLED BY A BLAST.—An inquest was held on Saturday last before Mr. T. P. Brown, deputy Coroner, touching the death of James Lashbrook, a miner employed in the tunnel, near Ingleton, on the new Settle and Carlisle Railway. After hearing the evidence, a verdict of "Accidentally killed by a dynamite cartridge," was returned."

The newspaper reports that James was employed as a miner *'in the tunnel, near Ingleton'*[1], the usual name for the Ingleton Fells. James would have been working at Blea Moor tunnel between Ribblehead and the top of Dentdale. Many other navvies died from dynamite explosions in this tunnel, but were buried elsewhere.

James' death certificate gives his death 'at Settle' so he had been brought back for the coroner's inquest. James is buried in an unmarked grave in the Ancient graveyard.

James' siblings also worked as, or married labourers and stayed in Devon and Cornwall. James' brother George died in the same year as James, aged 21. William's father lived to the age of 78, marrying his much younger second wife when he was 68.

·· ʃ ···

Robert Ralph, died 24th May 1874, leaving two orphaned children

There were six Robert Ralphs living in Settle at the time of the 1871 census, all related. Navvy Robert's parents were (another) **Robert Ralph**, a joiner and his wife **Mary Higson**. Robert (Jnr), born in 1833, had married **Mary Dale** from Skipton in 1858. They had three children while Robert worked as a stonemason, but a son, also called Robert, died in 1872, aged four. At the time of the 1871 census, Robert and family were living in Bowskills Yard behind Castle Hill in Settle, neighbours to young apprentice **Robert Henry Jackson**.

In a heartbreaking illustration of the impact of contagious disease, on 11th May 1874, wife Mary died. Just 13 days later, on 24th May, Robert also died. They were aged 42 and 41 respectively [1]. Such was the way of things in the 19th century.

> Settle.—On the 11th inst., Mary, wife of Mr. Robert Ralph, stonemason, aged 42 years.

> Settle.—On the 24th inst., Mr. Robert Ralph, stonemason, aged 41 years.

Robert was another casualty of phthisis (tuberculosis), disease of the liver and dropsy (oedema, swelling) and it's very likely that Mary died of something similar. They were buried in unmarked graves.

| Twenty fourth May 1874 Settle | Robert Ralph | Male | 41 years | Stonemason | Phthisis Disease of liver General dropsy certified | Mary Sewell Present at the death Settle |

They left two orphaned daughters, aged nine and eleven. Daughter **Ann Dale Ralph** was brought up by her aunt **Martha (Ralph) Sanderson** whose husband **John** ran the Talbot Inn in Settle. Ann died a spinster, aged 46, but spent her last 20 years in an asylum. Daughter **Mary Jane** was brought up by aunt **Mary (Ralph) Sewell** who had registered Robert's death. Mary had married **Aaron Sewell**, another stonemason, who had moved to Settle from Cockermouth, Cumbria to work on the railways. The

Sewells' eldest two infant children, **Thomas** and **Emily Alice**, died within five days of each other in January 1876 and are buried in the graveyard, hopefully with Robert and Mary. This prompted a move to Lancashire, with niece Mary Jane Ralph. Mary Jane had an illegitimate son, named Robert, but he died aged six. A year later she married **Sutcliffe Stott** who worked in the cotton mills and they had several children.

···JՐ···

James Harry Smith, died 22nd August 1874, another labourer and dad

James Harry Smith, born in 1836 in Leeds, was the only child of **George Smith**, a blacksmith and **Emma Ramsgill** who may have died when he was born. In 1863, aged 28, James married **Annie Frizzell** who was from the Isle of Man. Annie's father **Edward Henry Frizzell** was a sailor who died while she was a child. Sailors had a notoriously low life expectancy, even worse than navvies or military men.

Annie moved to Leeds to work as a waitress in the Albion Hotel at 142 Briggate. James and Annie married in Bradford and had a daughter, **Caroline Annie**, who died in infancy. By the time of the 1871 census James Harry and Annie were in Settle. James Harry worked on the railways but wasn't registered on the census return, presumably underground or on site. Annie was working as a domestic servant at the Golden Lion in Settle, for landlady *Mary Wetherell*. Annie had two sons while they were in Settle, both baptised at the church. **Sidney Charles** was born in December 1872 followed by **Harry** in January 1874.

On 22nd August 1874 James died, aged 40, in Settle. He was another victim of phthisis and acute pneumonia with wife Annie in attendance. James' death was certified by *Francis Green*.

After James Harry's death, Annie returned to Bradford and worked as an office cleaner whilst bringing up the two young boys. The sons worked as labourers, initially. Sidney became a barman. Harry married Olive Quirk and worked as a waiter.

···JՐ···

Samuel Henry, died 15th October 1874, an Irish stonemason

Samuel Henry was from Newry, Ireland, born in 1848, son of **John Henry**. Samuel's older brother **William**, a stonemason, had arrived in Settle by the time of the 1871 census. He lived in Poole's Row, Upper Settle with another Irish mason, John Moore, boarding with James Needs, an engine driver from Bristol and his family.

Samuel, also a stonemason, followed William to Settle and may have lived with him at Poole's Row. Irish navvies were in a minority and as such William and Samuel may have encountered more hostility than other navvies, this in 1872 [C].

> One point upon which they feel very strongly is their dislike to work with Irishmen. Scotchmen and Welshmen they can fraternise with, but an Irishman is enough, almost, to make a whole gang strike. These national feuds are of very old standing, and are supposed, by men who have lived among them for years, to be traditional.

Samuel died of pneumonia on 15th October 1874, aged just 25 and brother William was present at his death.

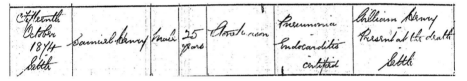

Samuel's younger brother **Patrick**, another stonemason, came over to Settle with him. Patrick married **Margaret Walsh** in Settle in 1877. Margaret was also Irish, from Tipperary, the daughter of a rag grinder. Patrick and Margaret lived in 1 Craven Cottages in Settle [H] to have the first few of their nine children before moving to Nelson, Lancashire.

> LOT 2. ALL THAT MESSUAGE, SHOP AND BAKE-HOUSE, situate in, and being No. 1 in Craven Terrace, in Settle aforesaid, with the Yard and the Out-buildings therein behind the same, and the Stable adjoining, now occupied by Mr. Patrick Henry.

Patrick and Margaret's son, **Henry Edward Henry**, died in November 1885, aged five months. Henry has the dubious honour of being the first burial in the 'Old' section of the graveyard in an unmarked plot, just in front of the church door. He is buried with two members of the *Bell family*.

Samuel's brothers are likely to have arranged for his gravestone in a quiet corner of the graveyard and may even have engraved it.

In affectionate remembrance of Samuel Henry of Commons, Newry, Ireland who died at Settle, Yorkshire, Oct 15 1874, aged 25 years. "Thy will be done"

···JᚠC···

Thomas Cooper, died 22nd February 1875, another Irish stonemason and Thomas Ferris, 30th April 1873, his sister's brother-in-law

During the early 1870s, **Thomas Cooper** (Snr), a 60 year old stonemason and his wife Mary moved to Settle from Newry, Ireland. They brought at least four grown up children and a few grandchildren with them. Their sons **Hugh** and **Thomas** (Jnr), born in 1852, also stonemasons, found work on the railway. Thomas Cooper (Jnr) died on 22nd February 1875, aged 23, another victim of pneumonia and phthisis from which he had been suffering for four months.

Twenty Second February 1875 Settle	Thomas Cooper	Male	23 years	Stonemason	Pneumonia Phthisis 4 months Certified by James Hartley MRCS	The Mark of Hugh Cooper Brother In Attendance Settle

Brother Hugh was present at Thomas' death. By the time of the 1881 census Hugh and his parents, aunts, other siblings and nephews and nieces had moved to Bootle. Thomas had a sister **Eliza Jane Cooper** who had married **Robert Ferris**, a greengrocer, also from Newry. Robert Ferris had a brother **Thomas Ferris** a labourer. The Ferris brothers had also found work connected to the Settle and Carlisle railway by the early 1870s.

Thomas Ferris, a railway labourer, had died on 30th April 1873, aged 28, after two weeks of inflammation of the lungs. Brother Robert was present at his death.

Thirtieth April 1873 Settle	Thomas Ferris	Male	28 years	Railway Labourer	Inflammation of the lungs 2 weeks certified	Robert Ferris Present at the death Settle

Robert and his wife **Eliza Jane Cooper** were a very fertile pairing. Their son **William** was born at 'Batty Wife'. It's hard to imagine what it must have been like to give birth under the shadow of Ribblehead Viaduct. Robert was a greengrocer who worked to service the navvy settlements at Ribblehead.

By 1873 the family had moved to Settle and by 1881 lived in the High Street — perhaps with the Cooper family? Eliza Jane gave birth to eight children, three of whom died in infancy or childhood in Settle. Daughter **Mary Jane Ferris** died in 1875, aged 17 months. Son **James Henry Ferris** died in 1880, aged one month and four year old **Robert Ferris** died five weeks later probably from the same disease. They could, hopefully, be buried with their uncles Thomas Ferris and Thomas Cooper.

After the birth of another son, **Robert Cooper Ferris**, Robert and Eliza also moved to Bootle, near the rest of the Cooper family. Eliza Jane died in 1896 in Bootle. Robert wasted no time in marrying the much younger **Mary Atherton** from Liverpool who produced another four daughters. Robert's children remained in Bootle scraping a living working on the docks, labouring and making match boxes.

Thomas Ferris and Thomas Cooper are buried together in the Ancient graveyard. The gravestone was erected in 1875 when Thomas Cooper and Mary Jane Ferris died.

In affectionate remembrance of Thomas Cooper of Newry who died at Settle Feb 22nd 1875 aged 23 years, also Thomas Ferris of Newry who died at Settle April 30th 1873 aged 28 years. Also Mary Jane Ferris who died at Settle aged 17 months. Not lost but gone before.

·· ·JⲒ·· ·

John Barrett, died 19th April 1875, after a life of hard work, and liquor

John, born in 1820, was from Hinton Charterhouse in the outskirts of Bath, the son of **Thomas Barrett** and **Mary Fussell**. Mary died two years after John was born, at the birth of a daughter, also called Mary. This was a family of agricultural labourers. Thomas spent the end of his life in Bath workhouse.

By the time of the 1871 census John was living in Poole's Yard, Upper Settle, working as a railway labourer with wife **Elizabeth** who came from Newton St Cyres, Devon.

| Nineteenth April 1875 Settle | John Barrett | Male | 53 years | Railway Labourer | Liver disease 9 months Ascites 6 weeks Certified by William Waltham M.B.S | The mark of Elizabeth Thompson Present at the death Settle |

John died on the 19th April 1875, aged 55, although recorded as 53. He died after nine months of liver damage and six weeks of ascites. Ascites is the build up of fluid in the abdomen caused by cirrhosis of the liver. John will have drunk a lot! John is buried in an unmarked grave somewhere in the Ancient graveyard.

The informant was a neighbour, 55 year old widow **Elizabeth (Cockshott) Thompson**. Elizabeth's husband, **Robert Thompson**, a stonemason's labourer had died ten years earlier, aged 52, leaving her to bring up five children, the youngest of whom, **Robina**, was born six months after Robert's death.

So, what happened to widow Elizabeth Barrett? Two years later, in Settle, Elizabeth married widower **James Gibbins,** a Bedfordshire railway labourer. James' first wife was **Tryphena Maidment.** At the time of the 1871 census James and Tryphena lived in the *'Ashfield Square'* navvy huts as the heads of the 'household' with six railway labourers as boarders. The Ashfield Square navvy huts were home to some 108 people: labourers, carpenters, stone masons, engine drivers, wives and children. The next entry on the census return was Rose Cottage on Bond Lane, formerly the entrance lodge to the Ashfield estate, and the vicarage on New Road (now Station Road).

James' wife Tryphena had died in 1874 and was buried at Giggleswick. The burial records describe her residence at death as 'Stansfield Square'. *George Stansfeld* and his wife *Sarah Birkbeck* had been the owners of the Ashfield estate until their deaths in 1869. The railway cut straight through the Stansfeld's nurseries and, obviously, the family received generous compensation. By the time of the 1871 census daughter Sarah Georgina married solicitor *Charles Henry Charlesworth* and lived at nearby Marshfield House before moving to Bank Well in Giggleswick. Daughter Rachel Wilhelmina married her first cousin *John Birkbeck* from Anley in Settle, by the railway cutting. At the time of the 1881 census Ashfield was the residence of Edmund Pearse Burd, West Riding's county auditor but he left in 1882. The Ashfield property became the Ashfield Hotel and more recently the Social Club.

By the time of the 1881 census, James and Elizabeth Gibbins had moved to East Ham, Essex where James worked as a labourer.

May all our navvies rest in peace *[C]*.

Whence they come, and whither they go, to shuffle off this mortal coil, when they have escaped the dangers of tunnels, cuttings, &c., few can tell.

The navvy is a very rough diamond; but when you come to mix with him familiarly, and to understand him, you come to realise that he is a diamond.

The Coroners, the Registrar and the Surgeons

The inquests into the deaths of our navvies were held by County Coroner **Thomas Brown** or Deputy Coroner **Thomas P Brown**. The registrar of the deaths was **John Cowburn**. Doctors **Francis Green** and **William Altham** were specifically named as certifying deaths. These men were from a very different part of the social scale to the navvies and so far more is known about them.

·· JГ ··

Thomas Brown and Thomas Parkinson Brown, the coroners

Thomas Brown, a farmer's son, was born in 1801 in Airton, Malhamdale. In Skipton, in 1837, he married **Mary Bradley**, an innkeeper's daughter and worked as a solicitor and coroner for the Skipton district. They had five children although two died in infancy. The only surviving son, **Thomas Parkinson Brown**, was born in 1838.

Historically, 'crowners' served the crown primarily to decide taxes payable at death. The internet tells us that, over time, the role of the coroner has evolved to *"conduct an inquest into the manner or cause of death that appeared to be of a suspicious, or unexplained nature and to investigate the identity of an unknown person who has been found dead. Coroners' inquests were usually held within the space of 48 hours following a death, as soon as the coroner could assemble a jury. They were held in a local public-house, municipal building or workhouse, but sometimes in the building where the death occurred. Some casualties were taken to the hospital, so the inquest would be conducted there, rather than where the person was living or died,"* which explains why some of our navvies are buried in Settle. The coroner usually came from a legal or medical background and tended to be appointed for life by the respective county.

Unsurprisingly, son Thomas Parkinson Brown was also a solicitor and 'deputy coroner' to his father. They were exceedingly busy men. A quick search of 19th century newspapers throws up literally hundreds of articles. They presided over the death of beer seller Christopher Wright killed by navvy Ellis Parker/Nelson, the many navvies killed between Settle and Dent and several victims of suicide who are buried in the graveyard. Father and son must have had incredibly strong stomachs. The newspaper reports of some of the deaths are graphic enough, never mind examining bodies in real life with associated odours. At an inquest held just one (warm) day after death, the body of navvy Thomas Burton was described as *"being in an advanced state of decomposition, the effluvia offensive and sickening to the jury"*.

Thomas (Snr) died in 1876. Son Thomas Parkinson Brown took over as coroner, a post he held for 40 years [3]. Amongst other responsibilities he also became the senior partner of *'Brown, Charlesworth and Wood'* solicitors so will have had close links with the Charlesworth family in Settle. Thomas remained single and died in 1905, aged 68, of a 'fatal paralytic seizure' [6]. He left a significant estate, worth well over £10 million in today's value. That's quite a contrast to the navvies.

SKIPTON SOLICITOR DEAD.

FATAL PARALYTIC SEIZURE AT HARRO-
GATE.

Edgar Wood, a partner in the business took over as coroner when Thomas died, a post which he held for 38 years until his death aged 82. An equal opportunities recruitment policy was probably not used for Edgar's appointment.

MR. T. P. BROWN. OF SKIPTON.

The death took place yesterday at Harrogate of Mr. Thomas Parkinson Brown, of Skipton, at the age of 68 years. He had been in failing health some little time. The interment takes place at Skipton on Tuesday.

Mr. Brown only resigned the Coronership of the Skipton district in December of last year, having discharged the duties of that office for over forty years. He was senior partner in the firm of Brown, Charlesworths, and Wood, solicitors, of Skipton.

Owing to the absence of his father (who was then Coroner for the Skipton district) Mr. Brown had to hold his first inquest when he was under age.

Mr. Brown occupied the position of Clerk to the Guardians of the Skipton Union and to the Rural Sanitary Authority for over a quarter of a century, and at the time of his death held the office of Superintendent Registrar for the Skipton district, and was chairman of the Skipton Room and Power Company.

He was a Liberal, a Churchman, and an enthusiastic sportsman.

·· ⅃⌐ ··

John Cowburn, the registrar

John Cowburn was the registrar for all the deaths of our navvies and so we have numerous examples of his handwriting and signature.

Signature, Description, and Residence of Informant	When Registered	Signature of Registrar
John Cock In Attendance Settle	Twenty Second May 1871	John Cowburn Registrar

John's father, another **John Cowburn**, had been an attorney and solicitor in Settle. With his partner Edward Norris, John (Snr) had dabbled in

LANCASTER & NEWCASTLE-UPON-TYNE RAILWAY.

RUMOURS having been industriously circulated to the prejudice of this undertaking, we beg to assure the Applicants for Shares that the intention to Abandon the Line never existed, and that every exertion will continue to be made to bring the matter before the ensuing Parliament.

COWBURN & NORRIS,
Solicitors to the Projected Company.

'railway mania' investments, but was declared insolvent when the railway planned between Lancaster and Newcastle upon Tyne collapsed [7].

John (Snr) had a painful death, aged 45, in 1855 whilst skating on the ice at 'Birkbeck Wear', near Anley [8]. The 19th century was much colder! In common with many navvies, John died from infection rather than from the injury itself.

MELANCHOLY ACCIDENT. On Monday, February 12th, an accident, attended with fatal consequences, occurred to John Cowburn, Esq., of Settle. He had been skating on Birkbeck Wear, and was about to finish, when he unfortunately went against a piece of rough ice, and fell heavily. His cheek was cut through under the eye. He was out on the Tuesday and Wednesday, but on the following Tuesday he was no more. It is supposed that Erysipelatous inflamation had spread fataly to the brain. He held the offices of Clerk of the County Court and Chief Constable for the Division of Staincliffe West, for which offices his Son is a candidate.

John's widow Jane (Cork) Cowburn spent the rest of her life running a confectionery business with her daughters on Kirkgate in Settle. In an interesting coincidence, at the time of the 1871 census, Jane was providing lodgings for **Robert Edward Wilson**, a 29 year old civil engineer from Leeds. This young man was the 'resident engineer' to oversee the building of the southern section of Contract No.1, the railway between Settle and Dent. At the same time, **Edgar Oswald Ferguson**, a 24 year old engineer was lodging with Margaret Garstang at the foot of Belle Hill in Giggleswick. Edgar was the 'resident engineer' for the northern section of the line. They both worked under the supervision of **John Sidney Crossley,** a 59 year old engineer from Loughborough, who delayed his retirement, despite a stroke, to tackle this project. Mr Crossley was in Leicestershire at the time. Despite Crossley's experience, it's incredible that the Midland Railway should entrust such a prestigious feat of engineering to two such young men.

Son John Cowburn (Jnr) was just 18 when his father died and he did well to continue the family business. He worked as an auctioneer, the Registrar of births, marriages and deaths and a High Bailiff. John married **Elizabeth Marsden Ayrton**, the daughter of the innkeeper of the Royal Oak in Settle and she gave him four sons, two of whom died in 1873, presumably from one of those infections rampant in Settle at the time. John (Jnr) had a premature and sudden death in 1876, aged just 39. The full account of the Cowburns' life is fascinating and is included in the Graveyard Project.

The Green brothers, surgeons to the Settle and Carlisle Railway

Edwin Septimus Green, born in 1843, was one of eight children of **Joseph Septimus Green**, a surgeon in Co Durham. Edwin qualified as a surgeon in Edinburgh, the most prestigious training college for medics at the time. In 1867, he married **Harriet Anderson** from South Shields and they moved straight to Settle, living in the large house opposite the Golden Lion Inn. They had three daughters.

Edwin was appointed surgeon to the Settle and Carlisle Railway for Contract No.1 district, including the Ingleton Fells and Batty Green. Navvies contributed 'threepence a fortnight' into a type of medical insurance scheme *[C]*. Facilities were minimal. In January 1871 Edwin and Dr James Hartley had to

> While in work, the men are made to pay towards the support of a doctor, who resides in or near the huts ready to attend in case of accident or illness. Usually the sum of threepence in the fortnight is deducted from the earnings, and for this, attendance, &c., is provided for wife and families.

> ACCIDENT.—Alfred Johnson, an excavator, employed in the construction of the new Settle and Carlisle Railway, met with an accident on the 6th inst., whilst at work in the "eleventh bridge cutting." The accident was caused by a fall of earth by which the foot of the poor fellow was nearly torn off. He was immediately after the occurrence, conveyed to the Hospital, a temporary wooden erection, provided by Mr. Ashwell, the contractor, and Drs. Green and Hartley were sent for who found it necessary to amputate the injured limb below the knee, which was accordingly done. We understand the man is progressing favourably.

47

amputate the lower leg of the unfortunate **Alfred Johnson,** a tunneller. There had been a fall of earth at the "eleventh bridge cutting" in which his foot *"was nearly torn off"*. The *'Hospital'* was *"a temporary wooden erection"* provided by the contractor [1]. Alfred would have been transferred to the hospital in the horse-drawn covered wagon. Let's hope they had some laudanum.

Edwin oversaw medical provision through the smallpox epidemic of 1871 which swept through the Batty Green navvy settlement, resulting in over 80 burials in the graveyard at Chapel-le-Dale. A temporary 'Smallpox and Fever Hospital' was opened, but was full within a fortnight of its opening. Of the 35 cases admitted in the first month, 19 were 'cured' and discharged; only three died. As the Medical Officer for the site, Edwin successfully applied to the Board of Guardians for another building to care for ten more patients and an additional male nurse.   After a jury's recommendation upon the death of navvy **Thomas Burton,** a *'dead house'* and washhouse were also added. Edwin would have certified the deaths of many navvies.

Edwin also served the Settle Union Workhouse in Giggleswick, another charitable contribution with little financial reward compared to his usual private patients. Edwin was only 27 when he died under tragic circumstances, being dragged by his horse for nearly a mile [1]. Edwin was given *"a full choral service in respect to his memory"*. Even though he was only in Settle for four years before he died, perhaps the manner of his death contributed to the decision to dedicate the beautiful church window to him at Holy Ascension? The window design includes the phrase *"He went doing good"*.

SERIOUS ACCIDENT.—An accident of a serious nature happened to Mr. E. S Green, surgeon, of this town, on Tuesday last. Mr. Green had ridden his horse to Swarthmoor, which is distant a few miles from Settle, and where he had some haymakers at work who were leading hay. The horse Mr. Green had ridden was being fastened to the hay cart, to be used as a trace-horse, when, before it got properly yoked, it suddenly started off at full gallop, Mr. Green having his legs entangled in a rope attached to the horse and was dragged along the road a considerable distance—nearly a mile—towards Little Stainforth, where, fortunately, the runaway was stopped by Mr. E Johnson, who was coming along the road in his conveyance which he pulled across the road, and succeeded in stopping the horse. Mr. Green was found to be very much bruised and lacerated, his clothes were literally worn through with being dragged and coming in contact with the road, and the flesh was torn from him in a frightful manner. Mr. Green was able to be removed to his residence the same evening, and medical aid was promptly in attendance. At the time of writing (Thursday)) we understand Mr. Green to be in a very critical state.

Widow Harriet, her mother and her daughters moved to Portsmouth although the bodies of Harriet and her mother were brought back to Settle for burial. Harriet's mother was one of the oldest people in the Ancient graveyard, dying when she was aged 92.

In loving Remembrance of Edwin Septimus Green, surgeon, born at Houghton-le-spring, Co Durham, Nov 13, 1843, died at Settle Aug 3 1871. Also of Harriet his wife who died June 22nd 1899 and of Harriet Anderson, her mother who died March 22 1904, age 92.

Unsurprisingly Edwin and Harriet's daughters married professional gentlemen. Daughter Emily married the *Rev'd Thomas Charlesworth*, son of the Settle solicitor.

This was not the end of the Greens' story in Settle. Edwin's brother, **Francis Green**, took over as railway surgeon. Francis certified the deaths of many navvies including those of **James Harry Smith** and **Robert Ralph**. As was the norm for professional bachelors, Francis resided at the inns in Settle. He is buried in the 'Old' graveyard. Francis' obituary states *"His reputation and skill speedily brought him a large and lucrative practice".* [3]

BOARD OF GUARDIANS.—At the fortnightly meeting of the Guardians of this union, held in the Board-room, on Tuesday last, Mr. Francis Green, in succession to his brother, the Late Mr. E. S. Green, was appointed medical officer for the district of Settle, Horton-in-Ribblesdale, and Ingleton Fel's; also to the small-pox and fever hospital at Batty Green within the above union.

OBITUARY.

We have to announce the death of Mr. Francis Green, M.D., L.R.C.P., which occurred on Monday, at the White Horse Hotel, Settle. After acquiring considerable experience as a practitioner at Newcastle, Dr. Green went to Settle about 20 years ago, and his reputation and skill speedily brought him a large and lucrative practice. His health had been failing for the past two or three years.

In loving memory of Francis Green, Surgeon of Settle. Who died Aug 25 1890 aged 53. Jesu. Mercy

William Altham, apothecary and surgeon

William [ph5], born in 1804 in Bentham, was one of four sons of **John Altham**, a well respected Bentham surgeon. William became an apothecary and, later, a surgeon. This was in the days of overlapping medical disciplines with physicians, (who had medical degrees to diagnose illness), surgeons (who conducted operations after a successful apprenticeship) and apothecaries (who made drugs to treat disease). In reality these roles overlapped and success depended on their reputation and popularity with fee-paying patients.

In the 1850s William made the move to Settle, taking over premises from *William Armistead* [SC] behind the Shambles where he practised until his death in 1880, aged 76.

MR. W. ALTHAM,

SURGEON, of GIGGLESWICK, embraces this opportunity to announce to the Inhabitants of Settle and the Neighbourhood, that he has engaged premises near the TOWN HEAD, SETTLE, the property of and late the residence of Mr. Armistead, Chemist and Druggist, where, on and after the 12th of May, he purposes practising Professionally as heretofore.

Giggleswick, May 1st, 1855.

William married twice: his first wife, **Jane Taylor,** was the daughter of the manager of the Higher Bentham Flax Mill. She died after the birth of her third child. In 1842 William married **Agnes Duckett**, the daughter of *Charles Duckett*, a successful farmer who had previously worked at the Folly in Settle. Agnes was 18 years younger than William and gave him another 12 children, at least, although Charles, Mary, Eleanor and two sons, both named William, died in infancy.

The influx of railway workers to Settle considerably increased William's workload. In 1871 William was called to attend to Christopher Wright, the 75 year old beer seller in Langcliffe who had been fatally beaten by navvy Ellis Nelson. William's testimony is detailed and thorough and makes it clear that Christopher's death was not due to natural causes *[1]*. In 1875 William also certified the death of our navvy **John Barrett.**

A report in the Lancaster Guardian remembered *"William was well liked and respected by the tradesmen and the working class. There was nothing about him proud and haughty and no doubt it was his uniform geniality which made him a special favourite with the mothers and their children."*

A further reminiscence in the 1920s explained his role as a dentist. He was described as *"a typical doctor of the old school, rough and ready, but with a wonderful capacity for healing."[CH]*

William, Agnes and their daughter Mary Eleanor are buried in the Quaker burial ground. None of William's children followed his medical vocation but several worked in the grocery trade and most moved away. Son **Thomas** worked in Settle as a grocer in the Market Place *[LSA]*. He married **Elizabeth Ann Morris** and they had five daughters before joining siblings in the north-east.

William Altham was then ca"ed and said : I reside in Settle and am a Licentiate of the London Apothecaries Society. I was called in to attend Christopher Wright on the 9th inst. I found him very much bruised There were two con'used wounds on the tibia of the right leg, the right thigh, and along the back were much discoloured.

I could not discover any disease to account for death. The injuries done to the brain and the kidneys, and the general shock to the nervous system, I consider to account for death. The external wounds were no doubt the cause of the internal injuries.

Doctors in those days were not so plentiful as they are to-day, and as for dentists they were an unknown quantity, at any rate at Settle. Dr. Altham was a typical doctor of the old school, rough and ready, but with a wonderful capacity for healing. Having a troublesome tooth I was sent by my parents to Dr. Altham to have it extracted. I went in fear and trembling, and I remember the doctor ordered me to sit on the floor and, getting my head between his knees, he inserted his " pliers " and, with a tug, out came the troublesome offender. With the tooth in one hand and my handkerchief, held to my mouth, in the other, I made my way homewards, " bleeding like a stuck sheep," as Robert Calvert put it, when I passed the Shambles. There were none of the arts of refinement of the dentist in those days, and yet the world went very well for all that.

◄ **THOMAS · ALTHAM,** ►
Grocer & Provision Dealer
MARKET PLACE, SETTLE.

HOME-CURED BACON AND HAMS
ALWAYS ON HAND.

English & American Cheese. Tin Goods. All kinds of Biscuits.
FINEST FRESH ROASTED COFFEE.

☞ T E A S :—2/-, 2/6, 3/-, 3/6. ◄
2d. off for 3 lbs., 3d. off for 6 lbs.
PATENT MEDICINES, PICKLES, JAMS.

TOBACCOS, CIGARS, PIPES, AND POUCHES.
Good Variety of Brushes.

M'Call White's Sheep and Lamb Dipping Composition.
Agent for the Queen Fire and Life Insurance Company.

··Jſ···

Winners and losers, richer or poorer, legal or 'creative', healthy or fatal

The navvies featured in this book and hundreds of others were the ultimate losers during the building of the Settle and Carlisle Railway. Society and the economy have been the beneficiaries for 150 years. Graveyard research has discovered several individual winners and losers.

The Railway Investors

Those with considerable funds have always made more money by lending to others and investing in business. After the success of the canals in the late 18th century, the railways became the next 'must have' investment. 'Railway Mania' was the leading speculative frenzy in the 1840s. Between 1844 and 1846, investments resulted in 6,220 miles of railway line — more than half of the modern UK railway network of 11,000 miles, which generally reaped healthy rewards.

There were several wealthy folk in Settle who made millions from investing in the railways, not least **Pudsey Dawson** who owned Langcliffe Hall, Marshfield on Kirkgate, the Folly and well over 500 acres of land in the area. However, not everyone was successful; as the price of railway shares increased, more and more money was poured in by speculators until an inevitable collapse. Around a third of authorised railways were never built as the companies collapsed, were bought out by competitors, or were fraudulent. The savvy investor put money into several companies to mitigate against this loss. We have already discovered that our registrar's father John Cowburn (Snr) had his fingers burnt in a bad investment.

Isabella Hargrave was the widow of *Stephen Hargrave* who had farmed the 2500-acre Stockdale Farm above Settle. She took advice to invest her inheritance in the railways. Letters to her son-in-law Adam Brown give an indication of the precarious nature of this *[A]*. In another she says, *"I saw Mr*

My Dear Adam

I was indeed glad to read the opening words of your letter this morning and could scarcely realize it would be true. The news was much too good after the past long months of anxiety and I fancy privation to very many poor creatures I cannot grudge the original share-holders their mites. Thanks to your forethought that I have not sufferred. I never for a moment dreaded misfortune coming to a good railway in that manner, but always thought them a perfectly safe investment, experience is at all times a good but dear teacher Will this years income due to me remain in the railway (?)ad stock and how am I to repay the £100,because it must be done I shall be very glad of the extra interest arising from the overdue <u>interest</u> in the railway, as I want to send Ella away to school.

Geldard and he said he should recommend us to invest £250 in the North Western Railway. He considered it perfectly safe. It is less interest than others but is it safe to risk so much in the railway? I shall be glad to hear from you."

Frederick Furlonger was a solicitor's clerk from Warminster who married Ellen, the daughter of *Charles Ratcliffe,* the manager of a Settle cotton mill. Frederick invested in the railways but, like many others, Frederick lost all his money. Unlike many others, he was so desperate that in August 1850 he embezzled one pound, 12 shillings from his employer in Woodbridge, Suffolk [9]. He was caught out and a catalogue of indiscretions was revealed.

During the trial it transpired that he had an alias 'Joseph Symonds' and had committed bigamy, already having a wife Sophia Brown (and a daughter), "a very foolish thing to do". The judge implied that Frederick had used a forged certificate to claim that he worked as a clerk for solicitor John Cowburn. This is John Cowburn (Snr), the father of our registrar, who had also lost money on the railways.

Frederick was found guilty. He was sentenced to imprisonment for one year, narrowly avoiding transportation. Frederick was then declared bankrupt in 1868. Incredibly, his two sons did very well out of life, one becoming a solicitor and auditor in Australia.

SINGULAR CASE OF EMBEZZLEMENT.—*Joseph Symonds* alias *Frederick Furlonger*, 31, a respectably dressed man, who took notes during the trial, was charged with having embezzled various sums of money the property of his employer, Mr. John Wood, of Woodbridge.—Mr. Power appeared for the prosecu-

Mr. Coburn then stepped into the witness-box. He said, I am a solicitor, at Settle, in Yorkshire. The prisoner married the daughter of a client of mine; during the railway mania he got into difficulties; his real name is Furlonger: he never was a clerk of mine.

You have been foolish enough to marry two wives—a very foolish thing to do—at the same time, what was still more foolish, you have been engaged in railway speculations, and lost a good deal of money. Under these circumstances, one ought not to bear too hardly upon a person who has tried to get back into a respectable situation, under such circumstances. Excepting in the matter before me, I do not attribute to you the idea that you came, through the medium of a forged certificate of character, for the purpose of cheating Mr. Wood. But the temptation seems to have come upon you whilst you were there, perhaps from distress owing to railway speculations. As I hope you are not wholly irreclaimable, the sentence is, that you be imprisoned and kept to hard labour for twelve calendar months. If I thought you had done this deliberately, I should certainly sentence you to transportation. But I do not. The prisoner burst into tears, and cried bitterly as he was removed.

··ɟ··

Entrepreneurs

The building of the railway was a tradesman's dream. Blacksmiths, stonemasons and joiners from Settle were suddenly in the right place at the right time. Coal was in demand as never before and the railways made it easy to obtain supplies [LSA]. **Abraham Smith** found a way into this lucrative market by marrying a clever businesswoman, **Sarah Ann Tatham.**

Sarah Ann, born in 1827, was the daughter of coal merchant, **Elisha Tatham** and his wife **Isabella**. Elisha died when Sarah was five and Isabella married another coal merchant, **Thomas Hall**, from Hellifield, who may have been Elisha's business partner.

After Elisha's death, Thomas worked in partnership with stepdaughter Sarah Ann. She ran a branch of the business in New Street (Station Road), Settle [SC]. Thomas died in 1858 and, undeterred, Sarah Ann continued the business with the help of half-sister **Mary Hall**. It was exceptionally unusual for single women to run businesses, especially one like this.

Abraham Smith was a cattle dealer and butcher from Bradford. By 1868 he had met and married Sarah Ann. Abraham was 28, Sarah Ann was 41. Marriages to elder women, especially by 13 years, were poorly regarded by society, but Abraham knew a good woman when he saw her! Abraham helped Sarah Ann run the business and took over when she died four years later in 1872. Abraham married another coal merchant's daughter, **Ann Wilkinson**, from Bradford.

S. A. TATHAM,

New Street, Settle,

BEGS to return her sincere thanks to the Public for past favours conferred upon her late deceased partner and herself, and to solicit a continuance of those favours. The business being now carried on solely by herself she hopes by strict attention and a good article to merit a share of public patronage and support.

The only Agent for the Habergham Coal.

TO THE DEBTORS AND CREDITORS OF THE LATE FIRM OF HALL AND TATHAM COAL MERCHANTS, SETTLE.

All persons having any claims or demands against the late Firm of Hall and Tatham, Coal Merchants, Settle, are requested to transmit the particulars thereof to Sarah Ann Tatham, of New Street, Settle, that the same may be examined and discharged. And all persons indebted to the said late Firm are required to pay the amount of their respective debts to the said Sarah Ann Tatham forthwith.

DATED the 30th day of December, 1858.

By Order,

G. & W. HARTLEY,

Solicitors, Settle.

Six years later Abraham died suddenly, just after the birth of their third daughter, Amy [1]. He was '*well known and generally respected*' which doesn't sound as good as it could. However, his estate was worth well over a million pounds in today's value, some of which he should definitely thank Sarah Ann Tatham for.

SETTLE.

SUDDEN DEATH.—On Monday morning last Mr. Abraham Smith, coal merchant, New Road, Settle, died suddenly at his residence. Deceased was well known and generally respected

The railway also provided opportunities for other types of entrepreneur . . .

Brothers *Robert* and *Worrell Kellam* found creative ways of making money on the railway. In 1878, Worrell Kellam, a railway joiner and foreman, was taken to court for fraud – he was taking on general labouring jobs and using his gang of men to do them whilst fiddling their time sheets so that their wages were paid by the railway [10]. The newspaper reports suggest this had happened before.

THE MIDLAND RAILWAY FRAUDS.

At the Leeds Assizes, on Saturday, before Mr. Justice Hawkins, Worrell Kellam (40), joiner, and Frederick Dark Jones (23), timekeeper, were again indicted for having unlawfully conspired together to obtain, by false pretences, from Joseph Smith, the master of Settle New Station, and the Midland Railway Company £3, and divers other sums of money, on divers other dates, the property of the Midland Railway Company, at Settle, in September last. It will be remembered that some time ago the Midland Company were found to have been systematically swindled to a considerable extent by their gangers, and others employed in making the Settle and Carlisle line. Westerman and Herrick, two foremen, were tried and convicted at the Manchester Assizes, the former being sentenced to twelve and the latter to six months' imprisonment. Kellam and Jones were tried early in the present Assizes, and were discharged. On Saturday, Mr. Fenwick, for Kellam, with-

Meanwhile *John Cook* worked as a carpenter on the railway. While working one day in 1877, he noticed Robert Kellam taking a piece of mahogany from the railway stores and making a puzzle money box with it [11].

THE ALLEGED FRAUDS ON THE MIDLAND RAILWAY.

At the West Riding Sessions at Wakefield, on Wednesday, a young man named Robert Kellam, a joiner in the employ of the Midland Railway Co., and brother to Worrall Kellam, who was recently committed for trial for conspiring to defraud the Midland Railway Co., was charged with having stolen six feet of mahogany, value 5s., the property of the company.—Mr. Barker prosecuted,

John's foreman at the time was none other than Worrell Kellam, Robert's brother. For some reason, Worrell sacked John from work and so, a

learned counsel.—After a short consultation, the jury found that the prisoner was "Not guilty, with a doubt." —The Chairman, in discharging the prisoner, pointed out to him that he had escaped by the skin of his teeth.

little later, John decided to tell the railway management about Robert taking the mahogany. The jury erred on the side of Robert Kellam, taking the opinion that John was bitter about losing his job and that there was no proof of theft. They found Robert *"not guilty, with a doubt"*. The chairman said that Robert had *"escaped justice by the skin of his teeth"*.

John Cook was the man who registered the death of navvy *James Burkinsher*. John had a son, also called John who was a church choirboy. In 1886 13 year old John (Jnr) died from drowning in the Ribble. He is buried just in front of the church door, just two plots away from Henry Edward Henry the nephew of navvy *Samuel Henry*. Robert and Worrell's poor mother Grace is also buried in the graveyard.

A catalogue of accidents

Newspapers reported hundreds of railway accidents and several were fatal. **Ambrose Preston**'s mother brought the family to Settle from Hellifield after her husband John died. The family scraped a living together with the men working as labourers. Ambrose and his brothers were often caught poaching to supplement their meagre diet. The railways provided a well paid employment opportunity for Ambrose, but at a price. By the sounds of it, in 1867, Ambrose had a very lucky escape suffering a compound fracture of the skull [3]. *"The unfortunate man, of whose recovery but faint hopes are entertained, belongs to Settle"*. Amazingly Ambrose lived for almost 20 more years. After his accident Ambrose and his wife, Elizabeth Young, settled in Settle with six children. The family lived in the Cammock Lane railway cottages and Ambrose continued to work on the railway as a platelayer.

SERIOUS ACCIDENT TO A PLATELAYER.—While a middle-aged man, in the employment of the Midland Railway Company as a platelayer, named Ambrose Preston, was at work in a sewer near the company's line at Leeds on Thursday afternoon, a stone, weighing about 10 lb., fell from a height of about 12 feet upon his head, and caused a severe compound fracture of the skull. The unfortunate man, of whose recovery but faint hopes are entertained, belongs to Settle, but at the time of the accident resided at 15, Water-hall, Water-lane, Leeds.

Phineas Butler and his sister **Mary Ann Butler** were the illegitimate children of Sarah Butler of Gargrave. She gave them up to a couple in Giggleswick who had raised several orphaned children. Apart from a couple of arrests for poaching, Phineas managed to survive without getting into trouble and found himself a job on the railway. In 1885, aged 28, Phineas married Matilda Frost, but less than a year later, in the snow, Phineas was involved in a fatal accident. The newspaper *[3]* seemed more concerned about the inconvenience to the passengers than poor Phineas, *"The passenger traffic is completely demoralised."* Within a couple of months Phineas' widow had left for New York with a tailor called Robert West. Phineas is buried in an unmarked grave with his sister Mary Ann and her husband William Heelis.

FATAL ACCIDENT NEAR SETTLE.

Yesterday morning Phineas Butler, aged 28 years, was clearing the snow from the points of the up main line at Hellifield Junction, when he was knocked down and killed. The Settle and Carlisle line was cleared on Monday evening, and yesterday the traffic was resumed, the passenger trains, however, running late. Towards evening the wind rose, and a second block appears to have occurred between Hawes Junction and Dent. The slow train due at Settle at 6.53 last night had not left Hawes Junction at ten o'clock. The passenger traffic is completely demoralised. More snow fell during the day.

John Goddard Barker was a professional musician who had moved to Settle from Ashby-de-la-Zouch to work as the organist at Settle Church. John was a bachelor and rented a room in Pen-y-Gent View from *Eliza Poole*.

John had recently retired when he was hit by a passing train in the night and died, aged 66 *[3]*. What was he doing on the railway during the night? John has a fine gravestone with a good view of the railway line. In one of those strange coincidences, the other occupant of this grave was Annie (Atkinson) Peberdy, granddaughter of the beer seller Christopher Wright, who had been killed by a navvy.

J. Goddard Barker
A.R.C.O.

Organist and Choirmaster at Settle Parish Church since May, 1903.

Teacher of Pianoforte, Organ, Singing, and Theory of Music.

A record of more than **50** pupils successful at Local Examinations (Practical & Theoretical) in grades ranging from Preliminary to Senior.

COMPOSER KILLED.

The body of Mr. John Goddard Barker, a North-country music teacher and composer, was found on the L M S Railway line at Settle, on Saturday.

Mr. Barker, who was 66 years of age, had apparently been caught by a passing train during the night.

Through Peaks and Dales [G]

In the year of '69 they planned to run a train
From Settle to Carlisle across the mountain range
They employed 3000 navvies to build this mighty road
Across the fells through Appleby that old steam engine rolled

Chorus: And it's up in the morning, lads, in wind, snow or hail
Hold fast your hammers, lads, and lay another rail

It's 72 miles from Settle to Carlisle
Across the roughest country in all the British Isles
They said it would take 4 years, but it took up nearer seven
In the first 20 miles it sent 400 men to heaven

They set up shanty towns to protect them from the cold
Inkerman, Sebastopol and Batty Wife Hole
And when they tired of women and the drinking of strong beer
They fought bare-fist style and they came from far and near

Now when the winter came, it froze them to the floor
It blew them off the viaducts and killed them on Blea Moor
Some died of the smallpox, some of cholera
Chapel and St Leonards have many buried there

Now if you ride this famous line across the heathered fells
When crossing Ribblehead viaduct remember the tale I tell
There's Mallerstang and Aisgill and Dent Dales lovely wilds
And navvy lads a-slavin' from Settle to Carlisle

Acknowledgments

This book has been generously funded by the **Friends of the Settle-Carlisle Line**, the **Settle and Carlisle Railway Trust** and **Stories in Stone**. **Stories in Stone** is a scheme of conservation and community projects in the Ingleborough area. The scheme was developed by the Ingleborough Dales Landscape Partnership led by Yorkshire Dales Millennium Trust, and supported by the National Lottery Heritage Fund. storiesinstone.org.uk

The Friends of the Settle-Carlisle Line (FoSCL) and the Settle and Carlisle Railway Trust (S&CRT) are partner organisations that take an active role in supporting the Settle-Carlisle line. FoSCL is a rail user group and a support group that puts a great deal of effort and

money into the preservation and maintenance of the Settle-Carlisle Line's unique heritage. The Settle and Carlisle Railway Trust is a charitable trust which helps to preserve, restore and maintain historic buildings and structures along the line and to promote public knowledge and appreciation of this much loved line. settlecarlisletrust.org.uk, foscl.org.uk

The money generated from this book will be used to support local charities.

Sarah Lister has railways in her genes. Her parents founded the Middleton (Heritage) Railway in Leeds. Her father, Dr Fred Youell, bought the last steam engine built at Stratford works, N7 69621, from British Rail and childhood holidays were often spent alongside the Settle to Carlisle Railway. After a career as a headteacher Sarah has found happiness with her husband in Settle. **Teresa**

Gordon retired to Settle in 2016 after many years working in education. She has two children and four wonderful grandchildren. Art was her passion at school and retirement has given her the opportunity to follow her dreams.

Since 2018 Sarah Lister has been researching the lives of those buried in the graveyard of Settle Parish Church, the **'Settle Graveyard Project'**. Sarah's first book, **'Curious Tales from the Ancient Graveyard'**, also published by Stories in Stone, is still available. Latest news of talks, graveyard tours and research is on the project's Facebook page. The project is ongoing and welcomes queries on **settleresearch@gmail.com**

Sarah's personal acknowledgements: This book is written in good faith with no offence intended. If I have inadvertently included errors or breached any copyright I apologise and would welcome corrections.

I'm incredibly lucky that so many friends have so generously supported the production of this book, despite the difficulties of 2020. Thanks to **Hannah Rose** and **Don Gamble** at Yorkshire Dales Millennium Trust for your continued support. To **Mark Rand, Martin Pearson, Paul Kampen, Mark Harvey** and the FoSCL committee, and of course to **Bryan Gray** and the Trustees at the S&CRT for your faith in this project. Thanks, again, to **Nigel Robinson** at iprint.

Immense thanks to the talented **Teresa Gordon** for her wonderful illustrations, cover artwork and her eye-opening perspective on the project. Thanks to patient proof readers **Hilary Brown, Sally Waterson, Beryl James** and **Pat Rand**. Thanks to **Rev'd Julie Clarkson, John** and **Edith Diggles** and **Paul Cochrane** at the church. Thanks to **Heather Lane, Anne Read, Caitlin Greenwood** of the North Craven Buildings and Preservation Trust at the Folly. Thanks to many other people for their ongoing support and encouragement especially Jim Parker, members of the original U3A team, including Eileen Bamford and the U3A committee. Most of all thanks to my patient, loving soul mate, husband and 2x great grandson of George Gibbs, tunneller on the Settle and Carlisle railway, **Ken Lister**.

Resources

The life stories of people with *italicised names* have been researched as part of the graveyard project and accounts can be found on dalescommunityarchives.org.uk. Research is based on findings from Ancestry and FindMyPast genealogy websites, Parish records at Holy Ascension and at St Alkelda's Giggleswick (by Nigel Mussett), Old OS maps at National Library of Scotland.

Newspaper cuttings with the kind permission of the *British Newspaper Archive:* 1 — Lancaster Gazette, 2 — Derbyshire Times, 3 — Leeds Mercury, 4 — Yorkshire Post, 5 — Rochdale Observer, 6 — Preston Herald, 7 — Kendal Mercury, 8 — Westmorland Gazette, 9 — Essex Herald, 10 — Manchester Evening News, 11 — Lancaster Guardian. CH — with the kind permission of the Craven Herald and Pioneer

Other resources: A — *The Settle and Carlisle Railway, Progress of Mr Ashwell's contract, B* — *"The Midland railway: its rise and progress. A narrative of modern enterprise"* by Frederick Smeeton Williams, 1876, *C* — *Chambers's Journal of Popular Literature, Science, and Arts,* 1872 'Railway makers', all three with thanks to *Mark Harvey, FoSCL, D* — Video 'The train now departing', 1986, comment by *Adrian Vaughan, E* — *Navvy settlements and the five contracts awarded to construct the line, Nigel Mussett, F* — Song lyrics *Karin Grandal-Park,* also part of the Stories in Stone Project, *G* — Song lyrics *Mike Donald, Through Peaks and Dales,* thanks to *Cate Holland, H* — with the kind permission of *John Reid, J* — with the kind permission of artist *Alan Fearnley.*

LSA/WSA — *Lambert's/Wildman's Settle Almanac, SC* — *Settle Chronicle* with the kind permission of the *North Craven Buildings Preservation Trust*

Photos: ph1 — *photo credited to Peter W Robinson, with the kind permission of Mark Rand, FoSCL, ph2* — *credited to Wikipedia, ph3* — *photo with the kind permission of Algy Metcalfe, ph4* — *photo credited to the descendants of the family on* ancestry.co.uk, *user ljelondon. ph5* — *credited to the family descendants via* ancestry.co.uk, *username Julie Boynton, ph8* — *Local photography by Ken Lister*